METAMORPHOSIS

MAKE THE CHANGE |
EMERGE MAGNIFICENT

SARA MADDERSON

For Chris, Paddy & Tilly.

You are my whole world.

CONTENTS

INTRODUCTION

Everyone thinks of changing the world, but no one thinks of changing himself.
Leo Tolstoy

Have you ever noticed that we tend to view children as unfinished people who are not fully developed, not wholly in possession of their full potential? At the same time, we adults perceive ourselves and each other as entirely complete and fully evolved, a finished masterpiece simply because we're in possession of a full set of teeth and our bodies have stopped growing - vertically, at least!

I don't think this complacency is warranted. We should *never* think of ourselves as complete. We now know that the brain can continue to re-form, grow new neural networks, and disconnect old ones throughout our lives. Where humanity is concerned, the old dog is far more capable of learning new tricks than most of us would like to admit.

We are evolutionary creatures and if we don't keep growing, we're missing out on one of the greatest pleasures of being human. However, I believe that we can take this one giant step further. Forget evolving; we can *transform* ourselves and our reality if we put our minds to it. *Metamorphosis* is the blueprint to take you through this process.

We don't tend to think of transformation as a human journey. Compare our slow evolution with the seemingly magical metamorphosis of a caterpillar into a butterfly. In its chrysalis, the caterpillar is safe and comfortable. By shedding the cocoon, it transforms into an extraordinary creature, possessing true magnificence. No wonder the butterfly has become a universal symbol of renewal.

Granted, we humans can't turn over a new leaf overnight, but we *can* choose to make our growth more a process of metamorphosis, less a passive evolution. We have the power to change much more quickly than society would have us believe, and I really believe that the extent of our transformation can wildly surpass our expectations. We all have an inner magnificence. We knew it as children, but our culture does a great job of clouding that inner knowing. We all possess beautiful, ethereal, powerful, kaleidoscopic wings. Now it's time to shake them out.

The Metamorphosis Metaphor: Diving Deeper

Transformation is a scary concept. As with most scary concepts, it's much more palatable when broken down. When I started my first company, the best advice I received was to view the launch phase as a series of tiny steps rather than one giant step. And that's exactly what we're going to do here. We're also going to spend half the book focusing on the *rewards* we'll reap through transformation, because they are immense.

First, let's consider what being 'cocooned' means. We're going to use the term cocoon interchangeably with chrysalis because it's less of a mouthful. I have no interest in writing a book about moths, but a moth's cocoon is a word that I suspect resonates more strongly with most of us than a butterfly's chrysalis. So I'm going to mix my metaphors!

For me, a cocoon signifies not only safety and comfort, but, more specifically, insulation from the realities of the outside world. It suggests a womb-like space where the familiar and known are celebrated and where we can be entirely oblivious to our unknown unknowns. It also implies a hiatus. For a caterpillar, a cocoon is a *temporary* refuge which is necessary to undergo total transformation. For us humans, however, we don't always feel the same rush to move on from its safety.

Snug and comfortable it may be, but a cocoon can be a form of captivity. Movement is confined. Visibility is limited. Possibilities are suspended. For those of us who've embraced being cocooned as a way of life, we may or may not feel stifled by this confinement. We may be painfully aware, semi-conscious, or blithely ignorant of the fact that we're in prison. But make no mistake: we are.

Contrast this with life on the other side of metamorphosis. I love the butterfly metaphor not just because of the seemingly magical nature of the transformation process itself, but because of what life looks like on the other side of that change. The two are inextricably linked. We can't have the rewards without the putting in the growth first.

I also want to address a common misconception. There can be a perception in the publishing industry that men write books for both men and women, while women write mainly for other women. This is not one of those books. Please don't worry that my choice of a butterfly metaphor means we're about to get airy-fairy. *We're not. Metamorphosis* is about the transformation of which we as humans are inherently capable, and this journey is equally applicable to both men and women.

Let's take a look at what life as a butterfly represents:

- **Freedom:** Contrast the comfortable confinement of the cocoon with the breathtaking autonomy of life with wings.
- **Perspective:** Butterflies choose their vantage-point over life. From their position, they can see the bigger picture and gaze into the distance. Their view-point allows them to focus on what brings them joy.
- **Re-definition:** Butterflies' past limitations (chubby caterpillar) in no way define their new reality.
- **Elevation:** Butterflies not only elevate their own lives but they elevate the experience of everyone who has the joy of encountering them.
- **Purpose:** While their apparent purpose is to revel in the beauty of nature, their very existence is purposeful.
- **Service:** Their purpose encompasses a host of services to our eco-system. They quietly, and unobtrusively, serve the world.
- **Innocence.** They are childlike in their gravitation towards what is most beautiful and abundant in nature. They are present and unencumbered.

It seems to me that butterflies have their priorities pretty sorted. Perhaps the most valuable lesson they teach us is that the process of metamorphosis is utterly worthwhile.

We're going to go on a similar journey (albeit with less eating than the very hungry caterpillar. Sorry).

My Own Metamorphosis

I am 41 as I start writing *Metamorphosis* and I've only been on my own personal growth journey for three years, ever since a friend recommended *Breaking the Habit of Being Yourself* by Dr Joe Dispenza. I devoured the book and, then aged 38, finally understood what should be a basic tenet of our existence: that **we do not have to live with the cards (or brains) that we are dealt**. We can overwrite decades-old patterns of thinking and behaviour and, in doing so, we can transform the way we live and effect huge change in our lives.

This won't be the last time that I mention Dr Dispenza in this book. He's reappearing in Chapter 1. But I'm grateful to him for reshaping my world-view so completely. Reading *Breaking the Habit* set me on a path to start devouring everything I could on related subjects. Why had I not thought to use my passion for reading to teach myself how to metamorphose as a person?

The truth is that it had never occurred to me that I could change, and by 'could,' I mean that I had the permission to change *or* that change was even possible. I was raised Catholic, and in my experience, if there's one thing that a convent education does *not* teach you, it's how to question. Questioning my faith or challenging my superiors were simply not options. Add to this my personality trait of being a pathological people-pleaser, who always wanted to be seen as a 'good girl', and I became someone who blindly accepted the status quo and was careful not to ruffle feathers.

It's really only in the last three years that I have started to question, and now the dam has well and truly burst. I had no idea how much fun it could be! Meanwhile, though, life does take over and it can be hard enough to get through the day, let alone live a conscious, healthy, spiritual, and fulfilling life. Daily life is *full-on*. I spent my 20s working on a trading floor, getting up before dawn for 10 years and working 12 hours a day. I swapped this for the duration of my 30s for motherhood and entrepreneurship - yes, at the same time; it was intense. I understand how hard it is to keep the balls in the air, and that reacting to life can take up all our bandwidth.

However, I got to the point where I woke up. That's the only way I can describe it. I felt as though I had been sleep-walking through life: exhausted, frazzled, reactive, unable to hold a thought, having zero clarity, and living in a way that was an inch deep and a mile wide. I have always been a dreamer and the lofty goals of an extraordinary life have always been there, but they started to taunt me as if the Grand Canyon lay between them and my daily reality. How, exactly, was I planning on getting myself from caterpillar to butterfly?

Metamorphosis is the answer to that question. It's the story of how I became conscious and actively chose to make big, scary, and life-defining changes. More importantly, it's a blueprint for how you can bring about whatever transformations you want in your own life. As you consume the lessons in this book you will consciously craft *yourself*, piece by piece, and therefore craft the world around you. That doesn't necessarily mean that anything has to change drastically in your life. It may be that you will choose to see your current life in a new light. To quote one of my favourite people, the late Dr Wayne Dyer:

Change the way you look at things, and the things you look at change.

Here are just a few of the ways in which I've noticed my outlook change. I've moved:

- From passivity to questioning
- From learned helplessness to self-responsibility
- From reactivity to purpose
- From control to surrender
- From dogma to spirituality
- From surviving to thriving

If any of these resonate with you, then read on. You'll find the tools you need in this book.

Redefining Success & Purpose

Most of my friends, former colleagues, and wider network are highly intelligent, dynamic, impressive, and wonderful people. Most of them have achieved high levels of success, if we define success by the traditional parameters of a great salary, healthy bank balance, and comfortable lifestyle. In short, their cocoons are pretty plush!

However, the continued sense that I get when I chat to these fabulous people is that they have the niggling feeling that there is something more. Their unknown unknowns are tapping at the edge of their consciousness. Like me, they have started to wake up to the realisation that our traditional definition of success may be off-balance.

This comes from both men and women. While I spent the last eight years running a fashion brand, dressing and growing close to incredible women with stellar careers and busy lives, my chosen industries of finance and entrepreneurship have given me wonderful friendships with smart, driven men too. All too often, we've channelled our energies and talents into building careers, families, and awesome cocoons. Many of us have omitted to devote the same focus to our inner world and our personal growth. After all, there are only so many hours in the day.

As my focus shifted, as my headspace increased after moving on from my fashion brand, and as I shared more and more of my frustrations and learnings with my broader network via my blog, I had clear feedback. We are all overwhelmed, no matter what our 'success' levels look like on paper. We all have days where we feel empty. Many of us compare our achievements to some future, indistinct, but ambitious goal and feel like we're falling short. We're stuck in 'when/then' mode: *when* I achieve X, *then* I will be happy. Meanwhile, life happens to us every day, but rather than life, it feels more like existence. *Metamorphosis* is my contribution to restoring equilibrium in the face of these conflicts.

Are You Ready?

If the path ahead seems daunting, let me offer some reassurance. When we consider the amount of work that nature puts into the metamorphosis process, we are reminded that we are not alone but are *co-creating* our transformation. Once we decide to view our cocoon not as a prison but as an incubator, we recognise how much of our progress can take place *inside* this safe, beloved place. This is a crucial element of the metaphor of metamorphosis; it's an invitation to trust the process. Trust nature to deliver. Trust what you are capable of. Lean into faith, and suspend cynicism. Be like a caterpillar; surrender, co-create, and enjoy the well-deserved unveiling of your newfound glory. There is an amazing force at work here.

This is quite literally the journey of a lifetime. It will take decades; there will likely be periods of growth, seasons of consolidation, and even stages of regression. That's fine, and normal. But as you grow you'll notice that your baseline edges higher. In time, your new normal, your new comfort zone, will exceed your previous dreams. Imagine a chart tracking your process. The line will not be straight; it will ebb and flow and occasionally dip, but it will show a clear upward direction as time goes on and you embody what you've learnt.

To be clear, I am on this transformational journey with you. Every wise word I offer is one that I need to hear too. I'm also figuring it out as I go along. Truthfully, I'm still winging it (pun intended). But life is about the journey, not the destination, and what a beautiful journey it will be for all of us.

HOW TO APPROACH THIS BOOK

I've created *Metamorphosis* in two parts. The first is dedicated to the steps that will deliver our own metamorphosis, and the second focuses on using our newfound strengths to take flight and create a life that we love.

I've designed these steps to build on each other. The steps themselves, and the order that they come in, are more art than science. As I revisited my journey so far and considered how to structure it for my readers, the steps fell into this sequence for me. However, you can of course read the book in any order, dip in and out, and revisit any sections that speak to you. So be irreverent with this book. Devour it, skip around it, and be sure to underline, circle, highlight, and annotate the hell out of it.

Here's how it's going to play out.

PART 1 - METAMORPHOSIS

1. Choosing Consciousness

I start this journey by making the case for why we should choose consciousness over our cocoon. I outline both the limitations of living at ordinary levels of consciousness and the incredible rewards that await us when we claim an extraordinary life as our birthright.

Once we wake up, the next step is ...

2. Taking 100% Responsibility

The foundational philosophy for any growth is to take 100% responsibility for everything in our lives. I believe that taking responsibility is the most empowering thing we can do. It allows us to re-write the script from victimhood to being the author of our own lives.

To execute this philosophy, we must know that ...

3. Self-discipline is the Key to Everything

Self-discipline is the #1 muscle that we must tone up in order to execute all of the new, exciting, and transformational changes that we will be making. This is a muscle that you can build quickly for amazing cumulative effects, and the ripple effect across all areas of your life is awesome and a lot of fun to boot!

The first area to put it into action is ...

4. Export Crap, Import Wisdom

Every day we can make the choice to entertain ourselves or to educate ourselves. Here we examine our power to decide exactly what we will and will not allow into our amazing brains. It's crucial to note that as well as *importing* wisdom we can *download* wisdom from within. We are already in possession of many more answers than we realise.

With clear minds, we'll be able to focus on our physical wellbeing ...

5. Fuel Up for the Journey

Optimising our health is a crucial part of our journey. For many of us, brain fog and energy slumps are the norm. We have become accustomed to seeing health as the absence of disease rather than the vibrant sense of vitality that we all can, and should, enjoy when our bodies are functioning as they were created to do. Here I focus on why we require optimal health to live an extraordinary life.

Once we've improved our physiology we're ready to take the final step of our metamorphosis ...

6. Farewell to Limiting Beliefs, Welcome to Limitless Living

What makes limiting beliefs so incredibly treacherous is that, most of the time, we have *no* idea that they exist. Therefore, we must chase them out of the shadows and become conscious of them. This is important, because limiting beliefs keep us in our cocoon and prevent us from seeing our true magnificence. When we change our narrative, life as a butterfly beckons.

PART 2: SPREAD YOUR WINGS AND FLY

I see this part of our journey as having three stages:

1. Before we fly off into the sunset, we examine whether we need to transform our perception of our *current* existence before we embark on building a new one (Chapters 7 & 8).
2. Necessary adjustments made, the second leg of our journey is how the heck to figure out what we want, which can be intimidating for many of us (Chapter 9).
3. The home stretch focuses on how to get from A to B, from our cocoon to a life of happiness and purpose (Chapters 10 & 11).

7. Perception is Reality

Before we draw up the life we *want*, we must look objectively at the life we *have*. Pulling the wool from our eyes is no mean feat, but when we do it, the effects can be miraculous. Chapter 7 will show you that our perceptions of reality have the power to transform our outlook on life.

One of the biggest inputs to our reality is ...

8. Love: Reframing How We See Others

I suspect that much of the upset that other people cause us is less to do with them and more to do with us. In this chapter, I suggest effective tools that we can use to overhaul our perceptions of, and reactions to, others. The shifts you make will not only improve the quality of your human connections, but will also stop you from being so eternally pissed off by everyone around you!

Having adjusted the lens through which we view our reality and our relationships, we're ready to ask ourselves the $1,000,000 question ...

9. What Do We Actually Want From Life?

When we're asked to paint a clear picture of our ideal life vision, many of us feel stuck. In this chapter, we'll activate the ability to identify what we want in life, to understand what will make us happy, and to ask ourselves the right questions. This process can be, and should be, so much fun!

Of course, we're only *co-creating* our lives; the Universe is our fellow creator. It's always worth remembering that ...

10. It's Not Luck, It's Synchronicity

Whether or not you're spiritual, I believe that the term 'luck' needs to be reframed. To believe in luck is to revert to a victim mentality. To believe in synchronicity, or in making one's own luck, is to take a much more empowered approach. Think of synchronicity as meaningful coincidences, or events coming together perfectly. Here we hone the ability to harness the power of universal forces or, if you prefer, simple human resilience, to take ownership of our lives.

The most familiar way of harnessing these universal powers is ...

11. Manifestation, Decoded

The concept of manifesting our desires is ubiquitous in the spiritual and personal growth arena, yet it remains a total minefield for many of us who feel pressured to master the skill of manifesting and inadequate when we seemingly fail to do so. This section is my bid to extricate the healthiest and most effective approaches to using manifestation. We've changed ourselves, and now it's time to change our lives.

So there we have it: eleven chapters to equip you as you set out on this awe-inspiring journey to elevate your level of consciousness, to metamorphose, and to craft for yourself the life that you were put here to live. I cannot wait to share these insights with you in more detail. Let's get started!

Along the way, I'll be referring to online resources for this book. I've created bonus activation exercises and suggested reading lists around each topic. These resources are free for Metamorphosis readers. I hope you enjoy them! You can find them all on my blog at www.healthywealthyandwiseuk.com/met.

PART I

METAMORPHOSIS

1

CHOOSING CONSCIOUSNESS

95 percent of who we are by age 35 is a set of involuntary programs, memorized behaviors, and habitual emotional reactions, it follows that 95 percent of our day, we are unconscious.

Dr Joe Dispenza, *Breaking the Habit of Being Yourself*

Here's my theory on why we tend to stick to a certain level of consciousness in our lives. It's not laziness or ignorance, it's a coping mechanism. The elephant in the room is, of course, that we don't ever know what the universe has in store for us or what lies around the corner. Quite literally, we have not a second of certitude ahead of us at any given moment. I write this less than 24 hours after a dear friend lost her husband to suicide. None of us saw it coming. Her life, and the lives of her children, have been irreversibly changed in an instant. We are puppets in this universal puppet show. We think we know the path that we are on, but that can change in the blink of an eye.

Is it any surprise, therefore, that we tend to play it safe? We bed down, lie low, and try not to 'tempt fate'. Choosing to wake up and live a fully conscious life means not only acknowledging, but *embracing*, the inherent uncertainty of our existence.

I should pause here and define consciousness. In the opening quote for this chapter, Dr Dispenza claims that we are pretty much unconscious 95% of the time. So what does it mean to be conscious? Michael Singer, in *The Untethered Soul*, writes:

 Consciousness is the highest word you will ever utter. There is nothing higher or deeper than consciousness. Consciousness is pure awareness.

While I find that quote inspiring, it's also intimidating. It conjures up visions of veteran Buddhist monks sitting high on a mountaintop, reaching utter transcendence. I'm not offering to lead you to the highest peaks of human consciousness, but I do think we can do substantially better than being on auto-pilot 95% of the time. I believe there's a middle ground where we can wake up to our purpose and lead a wonderfully fulfilling life. I also passionately believe that the quest for, and achievement of, a level of consciousness that enables us to feel awake, alive, energised, and empowered is one of the greatest privileges of being human.

Yes, it's seriously scary to walk away from the tried-and-tested and to embrace uncertainty. But the truth is that playing it safe in no way inoculates any of us from the vagaries of this thing we call life. Much better, I say, to choose to be the driver rather than the passenger in your life. Buckle up and enjoy the ride!

WHAT DOES IT MEAN TO LIVE UNCONSCIOUSLY?

This question has two layers of meaning. Primarily, it asks what is the definition of living unconsciously. More subtly, it asks what are the consequences of living that way.

Here are what I see as the faces of an 'unconscious life'. You may recognise some or all. You may feel degrees of these dispositions; they may come and go depending on the whims of your external environment. I'm not equating unconsciousness with unhappiness. It's possible to be perfectly content in life without elevating your conscious-ness to an extraordinary level. However, I do believe that this way of living has its risks, even if you would generally describe yourself as 'happy'.

Living unconsciously may mean that happiness or contentment is more fleeting, superficial, and ego-driven: the satisfaction of being right at someone else's expense, the impermanent thrill of winning, and the short-term delight of a box of chocolates. More troublesome, is that living unconsciously may cultivate regrets of opportunities wasted, of disappointments later in life, and, most commonly, of that vague feeling that there is something 'more' for which to strive, tangible but indefinable, and just out of reach.

As I break down the various faces of an unconscious life below, I also illustrate the implications of living this way.

The 10 Faces of an Unconscious Life

1. **Questioning little or nothing:** Questioning neither why you were put on this earth nor what your purpose is while

you are here. Taking the daily reality which serves as your definition of life at face value

2. **Being unaware of the bigger picture:** This is linked to our purpose, but awareness of the big picture is also a critical factor in differentiating humans from our mammalian relatives. If a dog sees a bone, he goes for it. If we see a chocolate bar, we may devour it or we may exercise our ability to choose the bigger picture: to lose weight or to stave off inflammation and chronic illness. Unconsciousness drives short-term thinking without much regard for any longer-term goals.

3. **Feeling numb:** Operating within a relatively narrow range of feelings and choosing not to rock the boat emotionally. Using props (alcohol, drugs, TV, sex, shopping) as anaesthetics when an unwelcome emotion (or any emotion!) does rear its head. The opposite is equally significant: you feel numb *without* the above props and increasingly need your fix to get your kicks. Related to this is:

4. **The absence of wonder:** The sunrises and sunsets pass you by; you register these shows but aren't moved to tears by their magnificence. You don't marvel; they're not significant for you. You may take the photos and post them on your social media feeds but the experience doesn't become a part of you; it's not the life-giving elixir that it may be for others.

5. **Being reactive:** While the absence of wonder is the defini-

tion that makes me most sad (because, what is a life without wonder?), being reactive is the easiest pitfall and therefore is the most common and insidious antidote to a conscious life. Furthermore, our ego will provide a million justifications for our reactivity. Life is intense. Most of us lack enough energy just to get through the day before self-medicating with TV and wine for the last couple of hours before bed. Just successfully reacting to what life throws at us feels like victory. In what parallel universe do we garner the perspective, energy, and *consciousness* required to create a life where we know what we want, we're alert to the magnificent opportunities that await us, and we have a roadmap to make them a reality? If you'd like to enter this parallel universe, read on.

6. **Living on autopilot:** We do so many things *unconsciously*. I'm no exception. While this is a nifty efficiency tool (I can quite safely drive my kids on the motorway while mentally writing this book), over-reliance on our subconscious means we are not really present. Where are we? Mired in our past or planning our future. If we're not present, are we really *living*?

7. **Monotony:** If you do the same things every day and react to the events and people in your life in the same way every day, then life really will not be a riot for you.

8. **Lack of understanding or awareness of others:** Unconsciousness puts us firmly at the centre of our own narrative. It prevents us from fully examining others' possible motives

or emotional states. This can damage our human connections based on the assumptions that we make, but can also cause us pain as it leads us to:

9. **Victim mentality:** Our internal narratives blame external circumstance and other people for any woes or failures. In this way unconsciousness equals disempowerment.

10. **Ignorance of our internal narratives:** This one is a biggie. When we are unconscious, we are unaware of the stories we tell ourselves, and we blithely accept them and build them into the fabric of life. We are going to blow the cover off these narratives in Chapter 6: Farewell to Limiting Beliefs.

What did you make of that list? Pretty depressing, eh?! If we go back to the second meaning of the question that I asked: 'What does it mean to live unconsciously?' then I think we can infer from the above that living unconsciously can result in reactivity, monotony, lack of wonder, social isolation or lack of really meaningful human connection, lack of purpose, a victim mentality, and powerlessness to name but a few. In a nutshell, it means missing out. It means missing out on life.

Life is not something that will happen tomorrow. It is happening this very second. What on earth is the point of being on this planet if we exist in an anaesthetised state? Very little, in my view. If this book has found its way to you then I suspect you are on the same journey as me. One of the affirmations I have recently started to say to myself (more on morning routines and affirmations later) is:

 My past is not my present. My life starts today, this morning, right this minute.

I love this affirmation because it's a wonderful way of wiping the slate clean. If you've had a shitty day the previous day, or a shitty week, month, year, or even life, then this mantra empowers you to *choose* a better, more fulfilling, purposeful way to live.

Here is the fun part. Each face of the unconscious life has its nemesis, the face of a conscious and fully-lived life. I found while I was brainstorming this second list that I was using powerful vocabulary, capital letters, and many exclamation marks! I hope that you too can feel the energy, strength, and potential in these words. They are vibrant, powerful concepts that draw us in and make us glad to be on this journey. These are the characteristics that you will learn to *embody* as you metamorphose.

The 10 Faces of a Conscious Life

1. **Curiosity:** This is both a cause and a symptom of a conscious existence. The first step to waking up is to know that you are asleep. By knowing that it is not only ok, but absolutely critical, to question everything about our existence, our *unknown* unknowns become *known* unknowns. I fully expect that many people living unconsciously are perfectly content, operating in a limited state of awareness, and blithely unaware that there is more to life than the reality that they've built around themselves. A useful illustration here is the 1998 movie, *The Truman Show*. Jim

Carrey's character is perfectly happy in the carefully constructed, artificial world in which he lives. That his world is a giant TV set is an *unknown* unknown for him. Only by getting curious and asking tough questions about what become *known* unknowns does he begin his quest for answers and for a life that he can live on his own terms. Sadly, the natural curiosity with which we're born is usually beaten out of us by grown-ups, social and cultural norms, and institutions. It's up to us to reclaim our innate curiosity and trade the comfort of our cocoon for an indescribable richness of existence.

2. **Purpose:** Purpose is a key driver of happiness. It gives our life meaning and substance, value and clarity. It's the difference between the three bricklayers in the old tale. The first believed he was laying bricks, the second saw himself building a wall, and the third held in his mind the vision of the beautiful cathedral he was building, an ode to God. All three men were performing the same role but derived hugely different value from it. Purpose is our 'Why'. It gets us out of bed in the morning and it allows us to elevate ourselves above our fellow mammals by choosing the green juice or the 5k run that we know will get us a step closer to our vision. If you exchange the bricklayer parable for a parenting one, it's the difference between seeing yourself as changing a shitty nappy or having the unspeakable privilege of caring for a beautiful, tiny, innocent human being. The fate of the human race depends on us all seeing the purpose in parenting. Purpose breathes consciousness into all that we do.

· · ·

3. **Vibrancy:** Vibrancy and vitality are what make you feel alive. They're the energies that pull you forward, they're the spring in your step, the tingle in your fingertips, and the sense of ebullience you feel just because you are alive. They don't require you to have a drink or do drugs or flex your credit card. These really are good vibrations; they're a sign that you are awake and open to life. When you allow yourself to feel these feelings, your ego may tell you that you are more vulnerable to getting hurt, when in reality, you feel stronger than ever. Revelling in the pure consciousness of being alive is one of the greatest and easiest natural highs available to us.

4. **Wonder:** For re-introducing me to the gift of wonder, I thank my children. Little children are wondrous beings. They are open to, and mesmerised by any manner of things, and I believe that this is one of the greatest lessons that children can teach us. They find joy in a cardboard box and magic in the dancing lights that a watch-face's reflection can make on a wall. But we don't need children to teach us how to wonder. Nature is the greatest source of wonder and is all around us. Great art, whether paintings, architecture, or music is also truly wondrous. Wonder and consciousness produce a glorious virtuous circle. When we allow ourselves to revel in wonder at the world around us and the humans who fill it, we feel ourselves becoming more conscious. Then, as we awaken, we notice so much more to fill us with wonder and awe.

5. **Proactivity:** The power of proactivity is a wonderful thing. The moment that we cross over from apathy and reactivity

to taking charge, to embracing our own potential and the potential of the day that lies ahead of us, is a moment where transformation can happen. When we are proactive, we take responsibility, we harness our energy in the most powerful way, and we assert that we are the authors of our own lives. We recognise that our strength is available to us to make magic happen when we choose to grasp the reins.

6. **Presence:** There is only the present moment. We all know this intellectually, but our ego is adept at time travel, transporting us to obsess over the past and anxiously mull over the future. 'Mindfulness' has become a ubiquitous catchphrase seemingly sent to taunt us and to remind us of where we are falling short. But with greater consciousness comes presence, and with increased presence you will feel fully conscious. Life is the here and now. By living on autopilot, we are missing it. Our senses have so many gifts for us when we choose to live in the present, gifts that are always available to us when we open our senses. Quite literally, we feel more alive when we stop to smell the roses or our children's skin, to listen to birdsong or to look at the sky. Presence is a present to our nervous system and our frazzled minds.

7. **Variety:** If habitual actions make up 95% of daily life, then it follows that that life must be pretty monotonous. We know that extraordinary events jolt us out of our stupor. One delightfully simple way to wake up is to shake things up. While travel is the greatest way to expand our horizons, any new experience will do. Life has *so* much variety to it if we reach for it. Take a new exercise class, listen to a new podcast, cook something from a region whose food culture

you know little about, change up your morning routine, walk in an unfamiliar park, or read an article by someone with precisely the opposite perspective from you. With each act you will open up the telescope lens a little wider and begin to see a bigger, brighter, and more beautiful vision of life.

8. **Empathy:** Someone who is conscious is more aware, not only of his or her own emotions, but of other people's. When we understand ourselves better, we have greater tools with which to build a rapport with others. While we're not privy to what goes on in each other's minds, the mere recognition that other people will necessarily have a different perspective from us affords us more empathy with and compassion for them. Not only does this create far better human connections and relationships, but, critically, it shields us from ascending the ladder of inference that so many of us climb far too easily (for example: 'She is being much quieter than usual, so she must not like me anymore'). Consciousness gives us greater intuition and makes us less likely to take other people at face value.

9. **Empowerment:** Consciousness puts us in the right mindset to co-create our lives with the universe. By taking responsibility for everything that happens in our lives, we wake up to our own immense power. For me, this is illustrated by the shift from asking why things happen *to* me, to asking why they are happening *for* me. When we're fully conscious, we see the bigger picture, we understand that our lives are following a path, and we trust that everything is unfolding precisely as it should. We have the wisdom to

trust that trials and tragedies are lessons, even if we know it may take a while to graduate from that class. Shifting from a victim mentality feels like climbing over from the back seat of the car to the front seat. You may be sharing dual controls with the universe, but you have the power to accept all of life's events and do with them what you will - that's true empowerment.

10. **Limitlessness:** The other side of this face, listed above, is ignorance of our internal narratives. When we put ourselves in a box built by other people, we allow ourselves to be limited. Whether we're actively told that we are not sporty or clever or attractive, or whether we infer those limits or conjure them up all by ourselves, we create artificial and totally nonsensical constructs for ourselves. By becoming aware that these constraints exist, we can start to blow them away. When we understand that none of the limits we've set ourselves really exist, we can allow ourselves to start *feeling* limitless. And that is the first step to *being* limitless. An affirmation that I say each morning comes from Dr Wayne Dyer:

 I place no limits or restrictions on all I intend to accomplish and become from here on in.

Our egos love to limit us. The universe has far bigger dreams for us if only we would open ourselves up to receiving them.

WHY WE NEED TO CHANGE WHO WE ARE IN ORDER TO CHANGE OUR LIVES

Einstein famously said, 'We cannot solve our problems with the same level of thinking that created them.' If the problems that we want to solve are rooted in the way that we think and feel, then it follows that we can't transform the less-than-ideal parts of our life if we continue to live as the person who created that reality.

Hal Elrod is the author of *The Miracle Morning*, hands-down one of the most life-changing books I have ever read. I am guilty of over-using the phrase 'life-changing' for books, but this book really has changed my life in that I now devote every weekday morning to waking up an hour before I need to, to devote myself to personal growth. Such is its power! You'll hear more about *The Miracle Morning* later in *Metamorphosis*, but, for now, I want to mention Elrod's premise, which gave me a lightbulb moment. The premise is this: we all have a life in our heads that we want to lead, and it's usually quite substantially different from our current lives (large bank balance, multiple vacation homes, body of a yogi – I could go on). Elrod's question to his readers is: exactly how and when do you think this is going to happen, if you remain mired in the same mediocrity every day?

His answer: to become successful, you first need to *become the person you need to be* to achieve this success. He says,

 I became present to the fact that I had not been developing myself into the person I needed to be, to attract, create, and sustain the level of success that I wanted ... We all want Level 10 success, in every area of our lives ...

but if our levels of personal development (knowledge, experience, mindset, beliefs, etc.) in any given area are not at a Level 10, then life is always going to be a struggle.

Dr Dispenza takes a very similar stance. He argues that if we spend our days in the 95% autopilot-mode to which we are used, it's very hard to action any great changes. In other words:

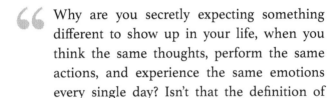

Why are you secretly expecting something different to show up in your life, when you think the same thoughts, perform the same actions, and experience the same emotions every single day? Isn't that the definition of insanity?

He follows up with:

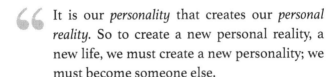

It is our *personality* that creates our *personal reality*. So to create a new personal reality, a new life, we must create a new personality; we must become someone else.

I buy into their theories. Let's say that today I am in Situation A. I have a dream of being in Situation B in 10 years. For most of us, A and B are light-years apart. On some level, I am hoping and assuming that this shift just magically happens. The probability, and the tragedy, is that it likely never will – unless I wake up one day and commit to undertaking the transformational growth necessary to be capable of making this shift a reality.

This growth will form the basis of the rest of *Metamor-*

phosis. I'm far enough into this journey to say with complete honesty that I believe we can re-create ourselves as the very best version of ourselves, the version in which we can write our own story and feel as though we gave life our best shot. I'm still very much on this journey, as it's an adventure that only ends on our deathbeds, but slowly the unknown unknowns become known unknowns, then known knowns as I take the steps I need to take to move forward. I'm delighted to be sharing these steps with you.

GETTING CONSCIOUS AND CURIOUS

Here is the reason that curiosity is important. When we're curious and we start to observe and question our behaviour, we start to become aware of how we are thinking, feeling, reacting and behaving rather than just letting our brains take us on a chemical rollercoaster. We have little power over our subconscious, but getting conscious about our thoughts and feelings is the first step to being able to intercept them, and therefore control them and change them.

In *Dare to Lead,* Brené Brown talks about getting curious as a form of reckoning. In the moment, when something raises our hackles or 'hooks' us emotionally, the key is to pivot away from the heat and get curious about what's going on. However,

 Whether it is a failure, a sideways comment from a colleague, a meeting that is full of disconnection and frustration, or a feeling of rising resentment when asked to do more than someone else, we're hooked, and we weren't taught the skill that the most resilient among us share: Slow down, take a deep breath, and

> get curious about what's happening. Instead,
> we bust out the armour.

She argues that we all have a physical trigger in our body that gives the game away for us when we get riled or emotionally hooked. It's our good old autonomic nervous system, taking us into fight-or-flight mode.

I want to share a story with you about when I got really curious with my emotions. It was a very trivial incident which stuck in my mind only because the force of my sympathetic nervous system's reaction felt way out of proportion. Here goes.

Last December we were on a Eurostar train with our two kids, headed to Disneyland Paris. Our carriage was packed. We had got on at King's Cross St Pancras, the first station, but there were two more stops before we went under the Channel. At the final British stop, with almost two hours of the journey left to go, a family similar to ours got on: harassed-looking parents and small kids. It turned out that Eurostar had allocated them the exact same four seats as us. They were perfectly nice and polite and British about it, as were we. As it appeared to be a case of Eurostar messing up and our being first-come-first-served, there wasn't a huge amount they could do so they struggled back down the carriage with their children to try to find more seats, or the train manager. We didn't see them again.

As I said, this was an utterly uneventful incident, so why do I bring it up? The reason it stayed with me is this. As they left, I noticed that my body had gone into full-on fight-or-flight mode. I was dizzy, I felt nauseous, I was shaking – it felt like a major blood-sugar crash which took several minutes to subside. My entire nervous system had primed itself for a perceived threat when there was none. So I got curious. What was it about the situation that had bothered me so much at a very primal level?

I concluded that my ego in turn had concluded that several things were gravely at risk: not only my and my family's comfortable ride for the next two hours, but my moral code and other people's opinions of me. My ego's instantaneous chatter went something like this:

'Oh God, we sat in the wrong seats. Now these people have come to turf us out and we're screwed. Oh God, we sat in the *right* seats (oh good, I was right) but this family is going to get nasty and try to accuse us of doing something wrong in any case. Oh shit, we have *both* been given these seats and therefore they're as entitled to them as we are, surely? Should we give them two of the four seats and put the kids on our laps? We should give them half the seats. Poor people. How come we got lucky and they didn't? It could have been us. Oh God, what if Tilly pulls a tantrum when she has to give up her seat? Shiiiiiiit. Why do we bother travelling with the kids again?'

This insight into the baser workings of my mind may amuse or horrify you. What transpired was that we got away lightly; the other family decided very quickly that they should go find other seats and we were left alone. But I was really shaken by what felt like a ridiculous over-reaction. It may seem that for me to get curious about this is an over-reaction to my over-reaction (yes, I exhaust myself). But here's the thing: what this interaction showed me was that my ego oscillates wildly between utter separateness – a binary us-and-them mentality, or self-preservation (they can't have our seats because then they will be comfortable and we will have to stand for two hours) – and the horror of being thought ill of by anyone, even people I don't know. I didn't want this poor family to think I was unreasonable by not offering them some seats, or to attack my morals in any way. I wanted to get the seats but I also wanted to be *right*.

My first horror had been that they were *right* and we were *wrong* – we'd sat in the wrong seats! The need to be right is such a big focus for the ego and no matter how many times I repeat to myself and my kids: 'It's more important to be kind than to be right,' it would seem that I need to take more of my own medicine.

In any case, I got away scot-free. We got to be *right,* we kept our seats, and we didn't have to confront or argue with anyone to get them. But the incident served as a stark reminder to me that I still have a lot of work to do on that ego of mine. I always find it fascinating that small children fight so openly about toys whereas on the face of it, we adults are so polite. For kids, it's not about being mean or badly brought up; it's completely primal. In their subconscious, they fear having that possession taken away from them because that could have meant life or death for their ancestors. And while we play nicely with other adults most of the time, our egos are busy keeping that sense of separation in play. If they get this toy, I won't. If they win, I lose. Totally binary.

The reason that I wanted to share this story is that if we don't get curious about these things, we won't get conscious of what is driving us. We won't question our motives or challenge ourselves to grow more. We won't have the opportunity to pause and choose a more noble reaction or emotion. We're so used to jumping on our moral high horse and citing principles. I sometimes think that if I was knocked down on a pedestrian crossing by a car running a red light, my moral high ground would get on the stretcher with me as I yelled, 'But I was right! The little man was green!'

Behaviour like this comes on a scale. It can simply be

the ego's thrill of being right, or it can easily spread to full-on road rage, for what is road-rage but moral outrage against any other driver whom you perceive to be behaving like a jack-ass? So while my behaviour on the Eurostar was perfectly acceptable by the standards of most people operating at a normal level of consciousness, I do think it's important for us to get crystal-clear about how we're reacting to life around us, why we feel this way, and what is the reaction we'd like to aim for next time something similar happens. By noticing and identifying our reaction we can often pause it and upgrade to a different emotion or reaction. This is what metamorphosis is all about.

There are two other big benefits to getting conscious and curious about our emotions and our reactions. Firstly, getting curious helps to diffuse situations like this. When you name your triggers, you realise there is nothing to worry about. On the Eurostar, there was no sabre-toothed tiger trying to maim us. No one was trying to steal our food. We were all good!

The second benefit is that it allows you to cut yourself some slack and be compassionate with yourself. I felt deeply ashamed after the poor, seat-less family wandered off; I felt slightly sickened in the same way that I do after I've yelled at my kids. But breaking down what had triggered me and how I'd reacted allowed me to do two things. Firstly, it enabled me to understand why I behaved like that (a combination of some primal, subconscious survival instinct that I couldn't quite control and the brattish reactions of my toddler-like ego which I do have more ability to train). Secondly, it offered me a real-time opportunity to observe and learn and *grow*.

David Hawkins, author of the astoundingly insightful

book *Letting Go*, says this about others, and I think we can give ourselves this gift too:

 We are able to see innocence even behind the most rash and apparently horrible behaviours. We look inside a person and see the frightened animal that just doesn't know any better.

By becoming conscious of our habitual thoughts and behaviours, we start to regain control over our ego. Once we're in control, then we have a powerful launchpad to make transformative, real-time changes across every aspect our lives.

You can check out my favourite books on this topic and complete the activation exercises for Choosing Consciousness at www.healthywealthyandwiseuk.com/met-book-bonus.

2

TAKING 100% RESPONSIBILITY

Do not give your attention to what others do or fail to do; give it to what you do or fail to do.

Buddha

This step is pretty straightforward. It simply requires us to take 100% responsibility for everything that has happened and will happen in our lives. However, simple in theory doesn't always mean easy in practice. So what does this mean in practice?

First, taking responsibility does *not* mean:

- guilt, self-blame, recrimination, self-loathing, or shame
- being responsible for what has been done *to* you by others

Taking responsibility does mean understanding that we can *choose*:

- all of our thoughts, emotions and behaviour
- how we react to everything that happens in our lives
- how we react to everything that others do to us
- how we can improve things going forward

It categorically does *not* mean shrugging off a wrong-doing or crime for example, or failing to stand up for ourselves, but it *does* mean owning the fact that this event is now part of our story and it means understanding that we have the authority to determine the direction that our story takes from here.

SHIRKING OUR RESPONSIBLITIES STARTS YOUNG

I believe we're taught to abdicate responsibility from a very early age, and this is something that I unknowingly fostered in my children when they were very little. Once I woke up to the implications of what I was doing, I changed my behaviour and my language immediately. Many of us will, when faced with a toddler who's run straight into a chair or table leg and is howling in pain and shock, attempt to comfort them by admonishing the chair: 'Naughty chair!!! Poor Tilly. Let's smack the chair.' And we duly smack the chair. Hands up, I've done this in the past. Once I started to read more on the perils of encouraging victimhood and to see more examples of fully-grown men and women failing to take responsibility, I quickly changed my tune.

I can't tell you how often I see adults lash out rather than take responsibility. I mean, it happens *every single day*. Once you become aware of this dynamic, you'll constantly notice adults behaving like infants who want Mummy to smack the chair. Dave trips over a child's toy on the floor and yells 'Who left that bloody thing in the middle of the floor? Tidy up your toys!'

I suspect, if we're honest, that our gut reaction may often be to respond like Dave. After all, when we trip over a toy we get a shock, we get embarrassed, we feel stupid, we feel vulnerable, and those emotions quickly turn to anger. Attack is the best form of defence, right? We feel threatened, our sympathetic nervous system kicks in, and we lash out, so we're often battling against both nature *and* nurture. I think there's true nobility in overcoming that gut reaction and choosing to take responsibility.

TAKING RESPONSIBILITY IN TINY WAYS CAN TRANSFORM OUR HUMAN CONNECTIONS

There are so many instances when we blame or shame others instead of holding ourselves accountable. Let me give you an example, also involving seat availability bizarrely enough, which shows just how deeply engrained in our culture the knee-jerk reaction of shifting responsibility is. Last Saturday night, my husband Chris and I took the kids to the cinema to watch a family movie. Ten minutes into the movie, two women came in with a gaggle of children. They went towards their allocated seats and found that another woman and her child were already sitting there. The late-comers loudly proceeded to tell the other woman that she needed to move. She seemed slow to either understand or accept this and a loud back-and-forth ensued. Meanwhile, a third woman started to speak up, accusing the latecomers of disruption. One of the latecomers then started arguing back.

Eventually the seats were vacated and the latecomers settled down to watch the movie.

As I watched this unfold, I could feel a very clear conflict in me. My higher self was trying valiantly to ignore the commotion, to give everyone involved the benefit of the doubt, and to think well of them (after all, their egos were likely experiencing the same feeling of threat as mine had on the Eurostar). My ego, however, wanted to give all of them a good slap. For God's sake, I thought, does everyone on this planet feel the need to go about every part of their life being entitled, morally outraged, and quick to be offended by absolutely everyone and everything? As I discussed the experience with Chris on my way home, he commented that interactions like this do make it difficult to be hopeful for the state of humanity.

But what if everyone in the cinema that evening had behaved like adults and taken 100% responsibility for their role? The latecomers would have quietly taken the first seats they saw to minimise disruption or they might have apologised profusely for disturbing the woman and her child already seated there. In turn, ideally she would have understood that her gamble of taking someone else's seats had not paid off and quickly vacated them. Most likely, both parties would then have avoided the sensation of righteous outrage that I'm sure they both endured for another quarter of an hour. And finally, the third woman would have had no reason to butt into the altercation or to believe that she had any justification to take offence.

In short, if everyone had had the self-awareness to consciously *note* and *over-ride* their base instincts, to *take responsibility* for their circumstances and react appropriately, one little cinema screening room would have enjoyed a higher vibration that evening. Elevating the human race lies in a million, tiny, individual choices for which we must all take responsibility. When we treat other people the way we wish to be treated, and in doing so acknowledge that we are all infinitely connected, then we strengthen our bonds and we experience more love and light.

WHY TAKING RESPONSIBILITY IS EMPOWERING

The tale above is intended to illustrate the ripple effects of failing to be accountable. I've seen the tension that arises in families when parents blame their spouses or children rather than taking responsibility. I've despaired that the 'Us and Them' mentality that we see fought out in religious wars and hate crimes is mirrored in a million tiny ways in our interactions with each other every minute of the day. However, I'm not here (just) to tug at your heart strings. I'm here to tell you unequivocally that taking 100% responsibility for your life and your behaviour is by far the best and most empowering thing you can do for yourself.

I'm not alone in thinking this. I was reading Jack Canfield's *The Success Principles* at the same time as I was scoping out the structure of this book. I'd already named this chapter and decided that it absolutely needed to be the starting point for the journey that I'm advocating. When I opened *The Success Principles*, I saw that the very first principle was 'Take 100% Responsibility For Your Life.' Great minds ...

Canfield shared an anecdote that I thought elegantly summarised this chapter's main lesson, which is that if you blame circumstances and other people for anything in your life, then you are telling your subconscious that you are a victim, as helpless and directionless as a leaf in the wind. However, if you are prepared to take responsibility for everything that manifests in your life and for every thought and action that you have and take, then you are hardwiring yourself to believe that you are in control of your life. While you cannot control circumstances or other people, you can fully control how you respond and take ownership of your story.

Canfield tells the story of how, soon after leaving graduate school, he had the good fortune to work for self-made multi-millionaire, W. Clement Stone. When Stone asked him one day whether he took 100% responsibility for his life, he wasn't sure how to respond. Stone explained that Canfield's only route to success would be to take total responsibility for all his results, successes *and* failures. He said:

 It is only by acknowledging that you have created everything up until now that you can take charge of creating the future you want.

You see Jack, if you realise that you have created your current conditions, then you can uncreate them and re-create them at will. Do you understand that?

In other words, you can't have it both ways. Bitching and moaning is hugely cathartic and satisfying in the short-term, but it's also extremely un-empowering. Imagine that instead of being mired deep in the shit-heap of your perceived problems, you are elevated to the refreshing position of being able to see what you are dealing with and to make informed decisions about the best way to move forward. It's called perspective, and taking responsibility is the first step in changing your perspective. Remember, when we change the way we look at things, those things change.

Taking responsibility for everything in your life is such a far-reaching and impactful philosophy that it will reappear in several guises throughout the book. For now, though, let's define responsibility as *accepting* and *owning* both our circumstances and our role in those circumstances. This equation illustrates just why taking responsibility is so empowering:

Acceptance + Ownership = Empowerment

In my head, taking responsibility means *accepting* everything that happens to me and taking *ownership* of what I do with it. Let's take them in turn.

Acceptance

This week, as I've been writing this chapter, I've been reading Hal Elrod's book, *The Miracle Equation*. I've already mentioned that I'm an enormous fan of his book, *The Miracle Morning*. *The Miracle Equation* focuses on how to implement a simple (though not easy) structure for achieving big results. When I read a certain chapter in *The Miracle Equation*, I laughed, for it was the perfect illustration of empowerment. Elrod says:

 Simply put, **all emotional pain that we have ever experienced, are experiencing now, or will ever experience in the future is self-created by our resistance to our reality.** Resistance typically shows up in the form of

> wishing and wanting something to be different that can't be.

Resistance is, of course, the opposite of acceptance, and what Elrod is saying is that, if we can accept everything that shows up in our lives, we will save ourselves endless pain and wasted energy. Acceptance is the first step to taking responsibility. This absolutely does not mean we have to be happy about our situation. Elrod was not happy when he was told he had a rare and aggressive form of leukaemia, but by accepting the diagnosis rather than denying or resisting it, he preserved valuable resources needed to move forward with what needed to be done next. This is ownership.

Ownership

If acceptance feels vaguely passive, then ownership is the essence of proactivity. It's a noble state, drawn from inner strength. Ownership is about owning everything from our identities and our narratives to our reactions and our goals. There are so many inspiring stories of people who have used tragedy to galvanise themselves to make the world a better place. You could say that they have turned 'bad luck' on its head and that what could have been a licence to fester on the sofa for evermore has become their purpose in life. I want to introduce you to Corporal Andy Reid, whose story was succinctly but beautifully told by Richard Reed (co-founder of Innocent) in his book, *If I Could Tell You Just One Thing*. (As an aside, this is one the books I gift most often.)

Reid lost both legs and one arm courtesy of the Taliban, ten days before his Afghan tour was due to end. Each year, Andy *celebrates* the anniversary of his accident, calling it Happy-Being-Alive Day. After all, the same IED had killed six of his fellow soldiers. *Change the way you look at things, and the things you look at change.* On each anniversary he sets himself a new physically challenging goal (most of which are far beyond me and my four operational limbs). The piece of advice that he shared with Reed was:

 At the end of the day I think the most important thing is don't look back on what has happened. Instead look forward to what you can do. Just crack on.

If this isn't a perfectly eloquent, and tremendously understated, way of encapsulating that acceptance + ownership = empowerment, I don't know what is.

The reason why taking responsibility is so empowering is that even when we feel that all other power has been taken away from us, the ability to choose how we react to and own our circumstances remains the very essence of what makes us human. There's a reason that *Man's Search For Meaning* by Viktor Frankl, a neurologist and survivor of Auschwitz and several other camps, is the most recommended book by so many people I admire. It's a deeply harrowing read, but the message at its core is one of positivity:

 Everything can be taken from a man but one thing: the last of the human freedoms—to choose one's attitude in any given set of circumstances, to choose one's own way.

Frankl had absolutely everything taken from him – his family, his freedom and his dignity. All that was left to him was to take ownership of his circumstances. He concluded that even in the midst of unimaginable suffering, his ability to choose his conduct and to find meaning in suffering was what in turn gave meaning to his life.

DENIAL IS THE BIGGEST IMPEDIMENT TO OWNERSHIP

When I was a child and a teenager, I overthought everything, and this led to bouts of extreme anxiety at a time in our society when there were very limited tools for managing this. I'll return to my anxiety at the beginning of Part 2, but I wanted to introduce it here because I found the most wonderful coping mechanism for anxiety – total denial.

Denial seemed to work brilliantly. Whereas my former approach to, say, a university application interview would have been to make myself sick with worry for days in advance, my new method was to block the upcoming event out completely and deal with it only when it finally came around. You'll be familiar with this tried-and-tested method: it's called burying one's head in the sand.

Of course, we know that repressing or denying our emotions instead of confronting them is extremely unhealthy. While I'm in a much better place these days, I still have my moments. Only the other day, my husband was driving down the too-narrow road that we live on (he's an excellent driver, by the way) and from my position in the passenger seat we felt far too close to the parked cars next to us. My solution? To close my eyes until we got home.

Somewhere, inside all of us, is that small child who remembers hiding under the bedcovers if our parents argued or being afraid to own up to having committed a small but naughty deed. Out of sight, out of mind. If we don't talk about it, we can pretend it didn't happen. Aside from the cumulative mental health issues that this approach is likely to cause, as long as we deny anything (whether our past experiences and actions or our current short-fallings or debts) we cannot fix it. We don't have an opportunity to tackle any shadows in our lives until we can bring them into the light.

I believe that there are two kinds of denial. The first is the denial that our problems even exist, which I've just mentioned. I believe it is closely and messily tied in with the second type: denial that we are responsible for our problems. Both types are unempowering and prevent us from taking any meaningful action to overturn our problems.

Therapist Lori Gottlieb wrote a wonderful book, *Maybe You Should Talk to Someone*, which made me laugh and cry and offered words of wisdom from her extensive experience with clients. She notes that:

 One of the most important steps in therapy is helping people take responsibility for their current predicaments, because once they realize that they can (and must) construct their own lives, they're free to generate change.

Gottlieb goes on to say that most people believe the majority of their problems are circumstantial, or 'not their fault.' I believe that when we deny that we *have* a problem, it regularly leads us to *shift* our anger or other negative emotions around that problem onto something or someone else – we are extremely efficient at transferring our emotions rather than, heaven forfend, dealing with them. This manifests in so many ways every day. The obnoxious woman at the checkout is going through a divorce. The guy with road-rage has just lost his job. One of the characters in Gottlieb's book presents as a jackass, but, in reality, is reeling from, but failing to process, an unutterable family tragedy. His coping mechanism is to deny this and accuse absolutely everyone else in his life of being idiots.

We can't own our future if we deny our past and present. While it's excruciating to take this step, it's also transformational and liberating. As Jamie Foxx said,

 What's on the other side of fear? Nothing.

Money: A Melting-Pot of Denial

Money is a prime example of the danger of denial and the power of acceptance and ownership. There are few people on this earth that do not have a complicated relationship with money – but that's another book. As someone who ran a small business for eight years in the very capital-intensive fashion industry, I know how stressful it is to have constant money worries. I also know how appealing it is to bury your head in the sand and avoid looking at your bank balance in these situations. I had many days like this. *Out of sight, out of mind.* Conversely, I know how much of a *relief* it is to pull up the dreaded bank statements, face facts, and start making a plan, because then we go from being passengers to being in the driving seat.

I remember several years ago, I had made myself (quite literally) sick with worry over the ill-health of our business and, in particular, the havoc that our wholesale business was playing with our cashflow. Running a wholesale business felt like being an investor in a Ponzi scheme. By the time we'd bought fabrics in advance, paid our factories, and waited the obligatory ninety days to be paid by the stores that stocked us, the cashflow gap could be six or seven months. When we were paid, it was never enough to fund the larger, subsequent rounds of orders and we simply never caught up.

Finally, one night I lay in bed with a debilitating sinus infection. I tossed and turned and drafted an email in my head to my business partner, Helen. I got up at 3am and wrote her a very lengthy email laying out the main reasons why we needed to pull out of wholesale, and why our business didn't require it. It felt *great* to get it down on paper. I slept like a baby for the rest of the night. Helen was completely on the same page and we closed down our wholesale business almost without a backwards glance, buying ourselves several more years of solvency and improved cash-flow. When I owned my problems, I was empowered to act decisively.

In my decade in finance, something I learnt from the powers-that-be at Goldman Sachs was how *fast* they acted when things went wrong. That firm does not hire ostriches. In 2001 and 2008, during unprecedented crises, I watched in awe at how these leaders redesigned entire divisions, ostensibly from a blank sheet of paper. Some of their most creative and commercial restructurings came out of crisis. Denial was not an option. These men and women accepted their circumstances and *owned* them. I'm grateful to them for the lessons that I learnt. Denial is unhealthy for our minds and unhealthy for our circumstances. Taking ownership is the only option.

I am on a closed Facebook group which has a financial focus. Within the group we have a culture of extreme transparency and support. Almost all of us have a financial story that feels shameful to us. But, as Brené Brown often says, shame is a social emotion and it cannot stand in the light. When we come out of denial and own our story, shame can't survive. One member recently admitted to the group that she had huge debts. In fact, her admission was that she had only just worked out what her personal net worth was (it was a large negative number). The sense of relief that she felt as she owned that number, shared her story, and laid out her roadmap to decrease it, was palpable. Now that she knows her number she can make her game-plan; she is back in the driving seat and she feels *great* about it.

As Stephen Covey, author of *The 7 Habits of Highly Effective People*, puts it:

 Until a person can say deeply and honestly, 'I am what I am today because of the choices I made yesterday,' that person cannot say, 'I choose otherwise'.

You can check out my favourite books on this topic and complete the activation exercises for Taking 100% Responsibility at www.healthywealthyandwiseuk.com/met

3

SELF-DISCIPLINE IS THE KEY TO EVERYTHING

Motivation is what gets you started, habit is what keeps you going.

Jim Rohn

WHY SELF-DISCIPLINE IS THE KEY TO EVERYTHING

In the last couple of chapters, we've covered assessing and upgrading our emotions, choosing not to respond to our baser knee-jerk reactions, and taking responsibility for our actions and feelings. Have you noticed what character trait all of these steps require? Why, self-discipline of course!

I like to think of self-discipline as **the inner strength to see and choose the bigger, long-term picture over instant, fleeting pleasure.** It doesn't mean being boring, pushing constantly, or having no fun. Instead, it means keeping your eye on the prize and seeing your big vision as more important than the immediate temptation. It's realising that all our actions have consequences and that winning the big prize consists of lots of tiny little steps – it doesn't magically appear.

In a nutshell, if you want to have an extraordinary life you'll most likely have to become an extraordinary person first. Becoming extraordinary happens in a series of moments: every time we make the right choice for ourselves and others. I believe that building my self-discipline muscle is absolutely essential to ensuring that I *truly live*.

I love how Hal Elrod addresses the issue of snoozing the alarm in *The Miracle Morning*. He really nails the implications of whether or not we choose self-discipline. He argues that when we hit snooze, miss a workout, or procrastinate, our actions affect far more than that moment. Essentially, we're programming our subconscious that it's ok to flake out on our intentions. Rather than building our self-discipline muscle, we're allowing it to waste. Elrod says:

 Every time you choose to do the easy thing, instead of the right thing, you are shaping your identity, becoming the type of person who does what's easy, rather than what's right … We must stop isolating incidents and start seeing the bigger picture.

Every Category in Life Requires Self-Discipline for Success.

It's going to the gym when we don't feel like it. It's getting up for the fifth time in the night to comfort our kids when we're bloody exhausted. It's choosing to dismiss something that our spouse does to annoy us, because *the bigger picture is so much more important than the momentary pleasure*. We can't snipe at our partner for the kick of it and expect to have a strong relationship. We can't neglect our kids and hope to build trust. We can't keep putting off the gym and hoping that the six-pack will appear.

Happily, I have some tools to share with you; tools that have worked brilliantly for me:

CHANGING YOUR MOTIVATION: TURN HARD CHOICES INTO NO-BRAINERS

The first tool is inspired by Tony Robbins and was a real lightbulb moment for me when I read his book, *Awaken the Giant Within*. Robbins' method involves *changing what we associate with pleasure and pain*. As he points out, everything we do is to either avoid pain or gain pleasure. He says that when people fail to follow through on what they think they want in their lives, it's because they 'keep trying to change their behaviour, which is the *effect*, instead of dealing with the *cause* behind it.' Therefore, we need to change the things to which we connect pleasure and pain:

 What you link pain to and what you link pleasure to shapes your destiny.

We can condition our brains so easily and, I'm telling you, this tool is magic. Let's look at an example.

A few months ago, Chris was found to have elevated levels of serum ferritin in his blood. This can suggest chronic inflammation or liver problems. Chris is a pretty healthy guy, but, at the time, neither of us were immune to a few glasses of wine several times a week. Instantly, Chris stopped drinking. He didn't drink a drop for five months. What's more, he didn't moan at all about it. I watched in fascination; his interest in alcohol had seemingly vanished.

What I realised was that in his head, Chris had transformed alcohol from being a pleasure to a pain. He saw it as a probable cause of his elevated ferritin levels and of his likely inflammation. Instead of being tempted by a nice glass of red after a tough day at work, he had such a strong conviction that it was harmful to his body that he completely recoiled from it (and he normalised his ferritin levels). The reason that Tony Robbins' philosophy is such genius, is that we're all driven by our *motivations*, and if we change our *motivations* we can change our *behaviour* instantly – there is no more conflict.

Self-Discipline is a Virtuous Circle

I have some good news for you. When you build self-discipline it *quickly* becomes a virtuous circle. Nike was so, so right. If you can get yourself to 'just do it', momentum will be your friend. Author Mel Robbins calls the burst of energy needed for that first, crucial push 'activation force'. If you can find your activation force, then it really is smooth sailing from there.

The reason for this is that once we find ourselves engaging in an act of self-discipline, we are overjoyed, because we realise we're empowered! We've taken responsibility to achieve the outcomes we want, we've made a positive choice, and we're now one step closer to that outcome.

This sense of empowerment is addictive. We feel relieved (that that self-discipline muscle existed after all, deep underneath the flab of procrastination and lethargy) and we even feel smug. Yes! We're allowed to feel smug! Come on – who among us is so spiritually evolved that we don't enjoy the odd smug moment? Feel the warm glow and then *keep moving forwards*.

I really believe that, in today's society where flakiness, apathy, and a lack of interest in the consequences of our actions can be the norm, the moments when we choose to exercise self-discipline are a wonderful reminder of our full potential. We know that we can be great; we catch a glimpse of it and that glimpse suffices to propel us forward. Each win facilitates the next. We feel galvanised and we pledge to continue the forward momentum. Sometimes it feels almost like an out-of-body experience. We think – check me! I'm doing another round of repetitions. I'm throwing back the covers and getting out of bed. I'm putting the biscuit tin back in the cupboard. Enjoy it, and most of all, *remember how good it feels.* Success in life is a result of the beautiful compound effect of making great choices again and again, moment after moment.

From Motivation to Habit

Let's revert to Jim Rohn's quote at the start of this chapter: 'Motivation is what gets you started, habit is what keeps you going.' This is a seriously interesting observation because it is *true*.

The beautiful thing about self-discipline is that if you have the motivation to start, the habit kicks in quickly. Habits don't require motivation (unless you're my eight-year-old son, Paddy; that tooth-brushing habit seems to be taking a few years to form). One thing that I find amazing about humans is how quickly we can create a new normal. I remember when Paddy was in hospital for two weeks. He broke his femur and was in traction; it was Christmas, our daughter was seven weeks old, it definitely was not a Christmas to remember. Suddenly all of the seasonal admin went out the window and this was our new normal. I went from being pretty high-maintenance to being over the moon when Chris came back from a low-grade local supermarket with a sandwich and a multi-pack of women's briefs for me. What was 'normal' had shifted for me overnight – even clean underwear had quickly stopped being something I took for granted during those weeks in hospital.

Here's a more current example. I've been practising The Miracle Morning ™ for four months now, at the time of writing this. At first it was tough – I had to make the shift from snoozing the alarm to choosing to wake up 45 minutes earlier than usual. Added to that, I also had to start my morning with exercise which was literally horrifying to me.

Fast forward four months. I now get up at 5.40 a.m., earlier than the 6 a.m. I started with initially. I spring out of bed. I do power vinyasa or HIIT with glee every morning before moving onto my meditation, journaling, and the rest. I love and adore my morning routine and I feel utterly crap and highly unproductive if I skip a day. My Miracle Morning™ no longer requires any willpower at all. It's a *habit*.

The really interesting thing about creating habits is that you can use the galvanising force of your self-discipline virtuous circle to 'habit-stack'. Habit-stacking is when we stack something we *want* to make a habit on top of something that's already a habit. Because the habit infrastructure is there, the new soon-to-be-habit can be slotted in much more easily. For example, now I automatically take my probiotics and drink a big glass of water as soon as I get downstairs for my Miracle Morning™. Both of these acts used to be very inconsistent for me. I've really noticed that my ability to embrace and integrate new habitual behaviour quickly and painlessly has increased significantly because I have a workable framework to slot them into. It's a virtuous circle.

James Clear, author of *Atomic Habits*, defines habits as 'behaviours that get tied to context.' Habit-stacking acts as an anchor and this is why it works so well. If you set a habit to do some pelvic floor exercises (important for you too, gentlemen!) when you're brushing your teeth twice a day, you anchor a new habit onto a habitual behaviour. He also suggests 'implementation intention', or stating exactly *what* you are going to do, *when*, and *where*. This makes it much easier to perform said habit because of the specificity of the intention. Vague goals are not goals.

Turbocharging Your Willpower

There's been a lot of work done to show that we start our days with a finite supply of willpower and that we work our way through that inventory over the course of the day. That's why we'll often capitulate and opt for junk food or a glass of wine in the evening. This is why I love my Miracle Morning™ routine. I choose to use up a big proportion of my willpower on performing acts that will benefit *me,* before anyone else gets a piece of me and chips away at my willpower.

The ways to get around fighting your willpower are:

- Do the tough stuff early on in the day. I will *never* carve time out of my mid-afternoon or evening to work out, so I give myself no choice but to do it first thing.
- Start with a low bar. If you struggle to do a full workout, start very small with building your new habit. As you saw, I am gradually bringing my wake-up time forward. Similarly, I've lengthened my workouts as I've got used to them so I haven't

really found it painful. Don't make the first step a massive one. Go easy on yourself.

The beautiful thing about making things habitual is that once they stop requiring much effort to implement, you free up all your willpower and 'activation force' to start on a new challenge! You've created a new normal for yourself, and the baseline to which you hold yourself accountable has risen. The implications of doing this consistently across several areas over time is incredibly significant for what you can achieve in your life. The more we can use self-discipline to galvanise ourselves, the more quickly and effectively we metamorphose and the more we see our lives transform before our eyes.

Self-Discipline is Very Scalable

The model I've laid out above looks like this.

BUILD THE SELF-DISCIPLINE MUSCLE DAILY, TINY CHOICE BY TINY CHOICE

DEFINE MOTIVATIONS THAT TURN THESE HARD CHOICES INTO NO-BRAINERS

USE CONSISTENCY TO DEVELOP ENTRENCHED HABITS THAT REQUIRE LITTLE DISCIPLINE TO EXECUTE

AND REPEAT:
USE YOUR FREED-UP WILLPOWER TO CONQUER YOUR NEXT AREA OF FOCUS

This really is a blueprint for metamorphosis. By reiterating this process again and again, you can see far-reaching effects quickly, across several categories. Bringing consciousness to those moments where you choose self-discipline over the easy short-term outcome is the difference between the cocoon and metamorphosis.

I find that when I split my efforts between different categories of my life, it takes far less of a toll on my willpower and I can make meaningful progress on several fronts. Let me give you an example. If I focused all my self-discipline efforts on just my health, it's very likely that I would throw in the towel. Making a commitment to run daily *and* cut out all grains *and* do my pelvic floor exercises *and* give up alcohol *and* drink eight glasses of water a day is likely to overload my willpower.

However, if I'm committing to a daily meditation practice as well as some improvements in my diet and I'm also making a choice to put my phone away when the kids get home and I tell myself that I will increase my word count by 20% per day... that doesn't sound too bad to me. They all occupy very different parts of my headspace and so I find that the willpower needed for each one doesn't cannibalise the others. On the contrary, I'm really just taking advantage of the magical effects of compounding.

You'll see self-discipline pop up throughout this book. It's an amazing foundational tool that reminds you that *you* are in charge and it's a breathtakingly simple mechanism for effecting serious and transformational changes in your life.

You can check out my favourite books on this topic and complete the activation exercises for
Exercising Self-Discipline at
www.healthywealthyandwiseuk.com/met

4

EXPORT CRAP, IMPORT WISDOM

The most powerful way I've learned to compress time is to learn
through other people's experience. We can never truly master
time as long as our primary strategy for learning and mastering
our world is based upon trial and error.

Tony Robbins

This chapter is about filtering and optimizing what we allow
into our heads. To kick off, I have a shameful confession to
make. My *Daily Mail* habit used to be so engrained that
whenever I opened up an internet browser, my muscle
memory would prompt me to type D-A-I to pull up the *Mail
Online*. In fact, this even happened to me this morning
despite my self-imposed *Daily Mail* ban over the last few
months. So none of us are perfect. We all have our guilty
pleasures. Chapter 4 is not about denying ourselves those
pleasures but about becoming more *conscious* about what

we allow into, and store in, those incredibly precious brains of ours.

The 'Five Chimps' theory states that the moods and behaviours of a chimp can be predicted based on the five chimps with whom they hang out most frequently. We humans are not sufficiently evolved to be immune to these effects either. This can be a good thing or a bad thing. I choose to see it as a *very* helpful tool that allows me to act like a sponge, greedily soaking up the wisdom of those who've gone before me. I firmly believe that the quickest way to learn and grow as a person is to stand on the shoulders of others and to cherry-pick the advances that they have made for my own benefit. Hopefully, as I do, I will be able to benefit others in turn.

Personal development author, Bob Proctor, famously said: 'Thoughts become things.' We are our thoughts. They determine our reality and they shape our future. So let's take a look at how we can make those thoughts the healthiest and most productive (and enjoyable) that they can possibly be. We live in a hyper-invasive culture and it's easy to allow society to violate the sanctity of our inner worlds. In this chapter, we'll work through how to implement measures and practices to optimise our intellectual growth and, even more critically, our mental health.

First, we'll look at tools for freeing up crucial headspace in our minds and getting rid of all of the utter crap that threatens to overwhelm us. Think of this section as a colonic for our brains. Once we've started to regain control of our minds, we'll look at how to import the wisdom that will help us to be and do whatever we want. Then, critically, we'll look at tried-and-tested methods for downloading the wisdom that we unknowingly hold inside ourselves. There are amazing riches lurking in our subconscious, waiting to be unlocked.

EXPORT CRAP

We live in the greatest age of information, which is both an incredible luxury and a huge burden. Our brains are overwhelmed and it can often feel as if our minds, and our waking hours, are not our own. No wonder we feel reactive much of the time, when responding to incoming noise is a full-time job. Therefore, before we can import anything of value we need to get out the jet-spray and clear out the cobwebs. Here are some ways to do it.

Filter Your Inputs

There's a reason that my *Daily Mail* habit is no more. This reason is that every time I visit the *Mail Online*, I suffer one of two negative emotions. I might read some lugubrious article about a missing child or a child who's plummeted to their death from a balcony while on holiday. Anything of this ilk is enough to send me spiralling into anxiety and vivid daydreams of the gruesome fates that could possibly befall my kids. Not helpful, and not healthy. The other reaction I tend to have is boiling rage, when I read either their right-wing drivel or their grossly-simplified health and nutrition articles which are usually, in my view, utter rubbish. So my advice on filtering your information is:

1. Keep it mostly positive.

2. Keep your intellectual standards high (a.k.a. no more *Daily Mail*).

Decide How Much, and What News You Are Comfortable Consuming

There are many people, including very successful ones, who simply do not read the news. I tend to be in this camp. My father is often horrified by how little I know about current affairs. He thinks my lack of engagement is irresponsible. In my defence, I do subscribe to the idea that even if you don't care about politics, politics certainly cares about you. I don't agree with burying your head in the sand. I do admire how many influential figures, especially in the US, are very involved with lobbying on behalf of critical issues like US border policy and gun control. I am very much on board with this.

However, if you aspire not to worry about what you can't control, then there is a strong argument for not torturing yourself with the daily machinations of politicians. Since Britain voted to leave the EU, the mud-slinging and posturing by our politicians on every side has been unbearable. The bitching, moaning, and ego-driven behaviour makes me sick. I voted Remain; we lost. There is little I can do to control the outcome of Brexit from here and so I'm just not going to devote much time or energy to absorbing the playground spats in Parliament. I find it the opposite of elevating to lean into these leaders, who do not inspire me. They are not in my tribe of chimps.

The 2016 US presidential elections showed us the power of fake news and, in a similar vein to the 2013 horse-meat scandal in the UK, reminded us all that we should be seriously selective with our sources. I only read and listen to the words of people whom I trust to have integrity. These words may be in a publication like *The Economist* or they may come from a public figure like Arianna Huffington. Either way, I cherry-pick my sources of information carefully. (As a note, there are at least two sides to every story and fewer absolute truths than we may think, so I do believe that exposing ourselves to the counter-argument to our beliefs is advisable, and we'll cover this below in the 'Importing Wisdom' section.)

To return to my previous advice of keeping my inputs largely positive, this is a tool that I find works for me. I do, of course, choose to know when outrage and atrocity are occurring. I want to be informed and I also want the option to exercise my voice in fighting these tragedies. I have the same reaction as everyone else when I see images of the bodies of migrant children washed ashore. I am sickened and furious. It's for this reason that I choose not to *immerse* myself in these narratives. I inform myself but I take care not to let myself spiral. I believe that I'm more use to my family and to society when I choose to feel positive.

Turn Background Noise Down or Off

We are so bombarded by noise that we've become immune. In the same way that parents become acclimatised to noise levels at kids' parties that non-parents would find frankly horrific, we don't realise how stimulated we constantly are. The other day, as I walked to the supermarket, I noticed a busker competing for my eardrums with both a boom-box and the drilling of some road-workers. I felt violated!

Thus is life in central London, and so now I am very mindful about what noise I choose in my life (my children have no volume control, sadly). I usually make sure that I have the radio off in the car, as I've noticed that it's on merely by habit and serves little entertainment purpose. Silence really is golden (I assume those lyrics were written by a parent). Seize your golden moments and turn off Spotify, the radio, the TV, and whatever other noise sources you possibly can, whenever you can. Embrace even brief moments of tranquillity as precious interludes in your day.

Turn Off Notifications and Reclaim Control

We are all bombarded by notifications from our phones, tablets and laptops. Unread emails, piles of WhatsApp messages, and social media alerts can give us anxiety and FOMO. Companies from every industry are desperate to get to us as consumers, and friends expect instant responses. It can feel as though we have given up control of our time.

One affliction I certainly suffer from is the feeling that I am always operating an inch deep and a mile wide. I'm so susceptible to distraction (and science has shown that chemically we are rewarded with dopamine when we get incoming notifications, 'likes', and the rest) that I find it near impossible to really get deep work done. As writing a book necessities a bit of depth, I've started to get much stricter with my time. As I write this page, I'm consciously putting up barriers against all the crap that is just waiting to derail me. My phone is on airplane mode and I'm sitting in a lovely private members' club where I don't have to think about anything but the screen in front of me. No doorbell, no dirty dishes to silently berate me. Instagram gets confined to specific times of day. Using the Screen Time function on my iPhone is always a good reality check for how much time I actually spend scrolling social media vs how much I think I spend.

We have all been very well trained by the big tech companies to behave in a way that benefits them. It's time to re-train ourselves and our social circles. My friends now get a reply on WhatsApp when it suits *me*. Let me tell you a secret: if you don't get back to people immediately, the sky will not fall. It is so hard to get our brains to focus in this crazy world; when we do manage it, let's not sabotage ourselves with pings and rings – let's carve out the time and headspace that we *deserve* to let our amazing brains show us what they can really do.

Meditation and Mindfulness

These M-words are ubiquitous now, but it's no coincidence that the huge ascendance of practices that allow us to quiet our minds has come at this time in history. Actively balancing out the obscene amount of 'noise' that we experience feels like pushing water up a hill. I have a daily meditation practice but I'm far from a pro and it's something I'm really committed to improving.

There are a million excellent meditation books and apps out there to help us on our journey. This is not the book to do that. My tuppence-worth would be that if you don't have any kind of practice currently then it may be worth trying a few things out and seeing what works best for you. Here are a few suggestions:

The Z Technique by Emily Fletcher

Emily's book, *Stress Less, Accomplish More*, is delightfully no-BS and extremely practical. It's the very opposite of intimidating. She says:

> The point of meditation is not to clear the mind. I would argue that the point of meditation is to get good at life … It's easy for

us to see that trying to stop the heart from beating is fruitless, yet we continue to try to stop the mind from thinking. Then we feel like a meditation failure and quit.

The Z Technique is an accessible form of meditation practice that begins with some mindfulness and deepens into meditation by way of repeating a simple mantra to focus the mind. Each session only takes around fifteen minutes, and can be done anywhere that you can sit and close your eyes.

Breathwork

Breathwork is simply the use of certain breathing techniques to activate desired states, from deep relaxation to great vitality. Given how relentlessly busy my mind is, I find vanilla meditation techniques difficult. In a single breathwork session, on the other hand, I found depths of sweetly tangible peace that elude me for most of my waking hours, alongside the most incredible natural highs. It was a total revelation. The beauty of it is that our breath is a tool that we have at our disposal 24/7. Breathwork may be worth checking out if you find traditional meditation inaccessible. At the time of writing, I do Richie Bostock's amazing breathwork classes on the Fiit app.

Apps

There are so many great meditation apps like Headspace, Calm, and others. Most offer a free trial so you can see if you like their style. My favourite app is the free Insight Timer, where I particularly love Tara Brach's vipassana meditation and Sarah Blondin's guided meditations. Sarah is a poet and artist and has one of the world's most heavenly voices (she sounds like a Canadian Julia Roberts) and her short meditations are truly like going back to the womb.

Journaling

Journaling has become a daily practice for me as part of my Miracle Morning (TM) and its many layers of value are just beginning to become apparent. I could (and possibly will!) write an entire book on journaling. You can find more information on how to use journaling for incredible results on www.healthywealthyandwiseuk.com/met. Meanwhile, for the sole purpose of exporting crap, let me say that journaling is to mental crap what colonics are to actual crap. Journaling has been called 'mental windscreen wipers' or 'mental toothbrushing.' You get the idea. Author Diana Rabb says:

 Whatever it is that you write, putting words on the page is a form of therapy that doesn't cost a dime.

Here's the gig. All that monkey chatter that fills our minds from dawn to dusk and beyond? Get it down on paper. Bitch, moan, act like a three-year-old, feel free to obsess over why so-and-so didn't invite you to their party. It's better out than in.

The most beautiful book on journaling for both creativity and for clearing out your brain (both deeply interconnected) is Julia Cameron's *The Artist's Way*. Cameron describes her concept of The Morning Pages, three longhand pages of whatever you want, as 'an apparently pointless activity' that acts like chimp-vomit. These pages allow you to take out the mental garbage. Once it's down on paper, your chimp can stop fretting.

IMPORT WISDOM

Now that we've managed to rescue our brains from some of the crap that tends to get lodged there, let's look at how we can fill up these beautiful vessels with mental nectar. To repeat a previous point, it's so important that we remember we can *choose* exactly what we want to take on board mentally.

The world is our oyster today. We can learn any language we want on Duolingo. The world of how-to has been revolutionised by YouTube videos. We can carry every single author we love with us on our Kindle. How to possibly choose?

Your 5, 50, or 500 Chimps: Mental Mentors

I've made it a habit to surround myself with as many wise people as possible. Most of these people don't know me and some of them are dead! Happily for me, their wise words are immortalised and readily available when I want them – thanks Amazon.

What Do I Want from My Virtual Chimps?

It's worth having a think about what you want to absorb from the people whom you let into your life and your brain. What particular brand of wisdom are you in the market for? Is it spiritual, emotional, practical or intellectual? Indian cookery or quantum physics? Life lessons or after-life lessons?

I love reading about all kinds of topics but for the most part my choices tend to fall into the categories that I've chosen to cover in my blog: www.healthywealthyand-wiseuk.com. Above all, I gravitate towards authors who love learning and who believe that we are here to learn, experience, and live as fully as we can. Here are some of the categories I've identified as focus areas for my reading.

- Personal growth
- Mind-body connection
- Nutrition and functional medicine
- Spirituality
- Productivity and learning
- Career-building and wealth-creation

Recently, I felt overwhelmed by what I had read and what I had on my to-read list. I built a spreadsheet and put everything I'd read in the last three years into categories similar to the above. It was a great way to see at a glance where my interests so far lay and where I should prioritise my reading going forward.

You may feel like your life is pulling you in a certain direction at the moment. Whatever direction that is, there's a book for it. When I read the words of an author whose work and life story I admire, I feel as though I'm absorbing some of that person's magical qualities by osmosis and it's a wonderful feeling. When I read Richard Branson's books I feel energised and invigorated and I internalise his 'screw it, let's do it!' approach to life and business. When I read Oprah Winfrey or Brené Brown, I feel their deep wisdom and wonderful humanity viscerally like a warm hug. I am open to and grateful for whatever these wise folks can teach me.

Your Real-Life Chimps

Real-life connections are just as important, if not more-so, than mental mentors. Here are my views on surrounding yourself with kindred spirits who will have your back and feed your soul.

- I see some of my friends as **my board of directors.** They have my back, they want to see me thrive, and they will call out my BS and tell it like it is. I hope I do the same for them.
- Spending time with people with the same hopes and dreams or the **same level of ambition for their personal growth** can make a huge difference to how motivated and well-equipped you are to grab life by the horns.
- I've found some great circles of like-minded people on **Facebook groups.** It's great to have tribes of people who 'get' you and from whom you can learn. A good place to start is to search Groups by keyword (e.g. Personal Development) or to join a group based around a book or course that you've done. The common journey I've shared with the people in my groups provides a wonderful connection from which to communicate our growth journeys as they develop.
- **New friendships can be intoxicating, revitalising, and sometimes as powerful as established friendships.** Nothing beats a friend

who knows you so well that you can be your true self. But I believe that special people come into our lives at just the right time and it's worth acknowledging the validity and blessings of these relationships. I once heard author Elizabeth Gilbert say something to the effect that you don't just *meet* a new girlfriend, you *recognise* her. I love this way of expressing the fact that your souls may have met before.

- **Friends should be reservoirs, not drains.** We are all highly intuitive creatures. If friends seem negative or give you a bad feeling, it may be a sign to reduce the level or frequency of your connection with that person. Our friends should be our cheerleaders and time spent with them should feel like filling our wells.
- **It's ok to move on from friendships**. It's not a sign that you are weak or a bad friend or shallow. It's a sign that two people may be moving in different directions in their lives and looking for different things from their friendships

Education not Entertainment

Whenever we have a spare moment, we can choose whether to educate or entertain ourselves. Entertainment is wonderful and offers us much-needed opportunities to relax, escape, and enjoy ourselves. Entertainment can also, of course, be wonderfully elevating.

When we've had a long day, we want to be entertained. I did note that for most of the decade I worked in banking, I watched and read pretty low-brow stuff in the evenings and on weekends. When you've been reading reports about interest rates and semiconductors all day, you just want something light-hearted.

Essentially, though, our free time is an opportunity to educate and elevate ourselves. When we spend hours playing Candy Crush or watching *Love Island,* we may want to evaluate the opportunity cost. Former Buddhist monk and social media giant, Jay Shetty, credits part of his astronomical following to the fact that he recognised the conflict we face when having to choose between education and entertainment. In an interview on the Mindvalley podcast series he said:

 The most successful people in the world – healthy, wealthy or wise, choose education over entertainment. The most unsuccessful people in the world – unhealthy, unwealthy or unwise – choose entertainment over education.

Shetty's answer was to create entertainment that was both educational and conscious. His social media feeds are elevating but are also peppered with the obligatory kitten videos – a healthy mix! In this way, Shetty made wisdom go viral.

Micro-Dosing on Wisdom

If we were to do a very detailed time-audit, we'd notice that lots of little chunks of time slip through our fingers. These make the perfect opportunities to import some wisdom. Even longer stretches of time, like a 30-minute commute, can easily evaporate into email-checking and Instagram-scrolling. Here are some suggestions for how to micro-dose on wisdom throughout your day:

- Keep inspiring books by the loo! We have a basket by the loo, and if a book makes it into that basket, it's the ultimate endorsement. I like books with bite-size content that I can scan in 30 seconds and receive a gem of wisdom from. Examples include *The Poetry Pharmacy* by William Sieghart, *The Path Made Clear* by Oprah Winfrey, and *If I Could Tell You Just One Thing* by Richard Reed.
- Choose a podcast over music if you're in the car, on the train, cooking, cleaning, or doing other tasks that allow you to focus on some auditory input (the other and equally beneficial approach is to turn off all interruptions and use these moments to be fully present). I love my wireless headphones, which allow me to listen to podcasts while I'm doing housework.
- Do a 5- or 10-minute meditation practice first or last thing in the day. Insight Timer allows you to filter meditations by how much time you have.
- Make notes or keep quotes from your favourite books in Evernote (we'll discuss this below) and revisit these favourite soundbites when you have a few spare minutes.
- There are so many journals, wall-calendars, and even loo roll with inspirational quotes printed for each day.
- Use an app like Blinkist to read summaries of non-fiction works. You can always buy the whole book if it piques your interest.

- Follow wise people on social media. I have one Instagram account that follows my friends plus chefs, interior designers, and fashion bloggers for more worldly inspiration. I have another account that only follows inspiring people of influence and I spend the majority of my social browsing time logged into that feed.

How to Maximise Learning, Understanding, and Retention

Sometimes I hear people mention that they're going to go on an information detox, to cut off the supply of information that they receive in order to focus on say a big writing project. This, to me, is even more hellish than the concept of a digital detox. I arguably consume *too* much; I read very fast and consume such a vast quantity of information that it's improbable to think that I'll retain enough of it as I go.

Therefore, here are some tips I've acquired along the way to allow myself to maximise the value I get from all this consumption.

- I read almost everything on my Kindle.
- I make a lot of highlights and export them to my laptop.
- I make a note in Evernote for each book I read and paste the highlights in so they are available on my devices whenever I need them.
- I go back through key books and make manual notes on the main lessons and messages that I've taken from them. These have grown into the book reviews on my blog, www.healthywealthyandwiseuk.com and are

usually in bullet format with lessons learnt, things I loved, and my Top 10 quotes. This way I have the absolute best bits of each book easily packaged for future reference.

- Taking these steps really helps me to consolidate and embed my learning. Because they're time-consuming, I only make manual notes and write book reviews on my favourite books so I can better internalise them.
- I check in on my notes from time to time, when I'm in need of an inspirational micro-dose.
- Podcasts: I make notes of the key takeaways in Evernote. I even do this on sun loungers!
- I sometimes buy books in both written and audio format. I did this with Dr Wayne Dyer's *The Power of Intention.* I learn and recall visually, but hearing him speak his message himself enhances my ability to emotionally internalise his teachings.

There are two other effective techniques that I want to share with you:

Brute Force Learning: This is a concept from memory coach Jonathan Levi, author of *The Only Skill That Matters.* It's immersive learning using many media. So, to learn a language, I may do an online course but also use Duolingo, meet with locals, read books, magazines, websites, watch movies, watch YouTube videos, and listen to podcasts. It not only accelerates the learning progress but also deepens understanding and improves your memory of what you're learning.

Reading Both Sides of the Story. I love it when students have to prep for both sides of a debate, not knowing which side they will have to argue. Most of us are guilty of confirmation bias, a.k.a. consuming material that we know will reaffirm our current beliefs. I would hazard a guess that many of our viewpoints can be simplistic at best or blinkered at worst. I know mine are. However, the older I get, the less black and white I am about life. Life is complex and nuanced, so consuming information that has a different (or opposite) perspective from ours can be eye-opening. Doing so will make us more intelligent, more thoughtful, and possibly even more empathetic to our fellow humans!

DOWNLOAD WISDOM

There is something that I very much want you to know, and that is that we all have a vast well of wisdom within us. The times I've been able to tap into mine are those moments when I can change my perspective. I suspect that much of the sensation of feeling lost, conflicted, or overwhelmed is because it is so hard for us to get a fresh perspective. We are stuck inside our own heads – in this particular environment, at this precise point in our personal timeline – and so it's difficult to have a perspective that comes from anything other than that physical reality. When we are able to shift that perspective to another reality within our own lives, or to tap into a field that's greater than ourselves, magic happens.

Below are some methods to allow you to download the

wisdom in your subconscious and to tap into the Universal consciousness.

Travel Forward in Time

A very effective method of shifting perspective is to travel forward in time in your head until you're at a ripe old age, say 85 years old. Close your eyes, take some deep breaths, and visualise how that feels. The key is to imagine that you have fulfilled your dreams. You have led the life you wanted to lead, rich with purpose and happiness. You have lived well and you are perfectly content with the magnificent life you created.

This wise, accomplished, fully self-actualised 85-year-old self is going to write a letter to your current self. You can take a moment before writing, but I suspect the pen will flow once you get started. Your future self is, above all, full of love and compassion for your current self. He or she remembers and feels your pain and struggles but, with the benefit of years of hindsight and perspective, he or she knows that everything will be ok.

The role of this letter is to celebrate what you have achieved so far and to let you know that the problems you are facing now are not insurmountable. Its other function is to give you a roadmap. If your future self shares with you what they have achieved, you will more clearly see the steps needed to get there. This can be an incredibly life-affirming and emotional experience to go through and is also a wonderful way to channel our capacity for self-love.

Travel Back in Time

If you need some perspective on how you're doing in life at the moment, whether you're making progress, hitting your goals, or in the right city, relationship, or job, why don't you go back in time and ask your younger self for some perspective?

So often, we are unhappy in the now because we compare *right now* to where we *want* to get to. We earn X and we want to earn Y. Too rarely do we do the opposite and look backwards to appreciate how far we've come. Entrepreneurial coach Dan Sullivan calls this 'the reverse gap', and I came across this cool idea in *The Code of the Extraordinary Mind*. When you measure against what you have yet to achieve, you'll usually be dissatisfied. However, when you take the time to appreciate how far you've come, you're much more likely to feel grateful.

We often take our achievements for granted. When we're goal-oriented, hitting one goal can mean moving straight onto the next one instead of pausing to take stock. When I was running my fashion company, it was all too easy to focus on how much we had yet to achieve, especially in terms of scale. However, sometimes in the middle of an enjoyable task like playing with fabric swatches or art-directing a beautiful photo shoot, I would stop and think of my 10-year-old self who was art-mad. How proud this little girl would be! Her only access to the dream-world of fashion was glossy magazines and the occasional shopping trip to Brown Thomas' department store in Dublin on a Saturday. The reality that I had achieved, while falling short of my current self's lofty ambitions, would dazzle this imaginative little girl who could only dream of being a real-life fashion designer in London.

Change the way you look at things, and the things you look at change.

Tap into the Power of Universal Intelligence.

Whether or not you are spiritual, there exists a consensus of a kind of universal intelligence. In the same way that an acorn has the 'knowing' needed to transform into an oak tree, we humans grow from an embryo to a fully-developed adult. This knowledge is innate, but many people believe that a further universal intelligence is at work, and that by aligning ourselves with it, we can co-create our world.

Dr Wayne Dyer calls these people 'connectors' and calls the force at work 'the power of intention.' In his wonderful book of the same name, he describes the energy field of intention and argues that we can all connect to it when needed, in the same way that we can grab a hand strap on a fast-moving tube or train when we need support on our journey. We can activate the power of intention by over-riding our egos, which are the main reason we're disconnected from intention in the first place. Essentially, connection to source comes through surrender.

When we need a helping hand and an injection of wisdom, we are better off surrendering to universal intelligence than we are digging our heels in and struggling on alone. Many people commonly perceived to be geniuses have claimed to have had little involvement with their moments of creative brilliance, insisting instead that they received these ideas as (often fully-baked) downloads from the universe. Even as I read through and edit this book, the paragraphs I like the most are the ones I don't remember writing.

This is a big topic and one to revisit in full at the end of the book when we dive into manifesting. However, the main message from Dr Dyer and other teachers is that if the universe is always sending an endless stream of wisdom and abundance, then to access it we simply need to *allow*. Of course, not many of us are that good at allowing!

I'll leave this topic with this beautiful prayer of surrender from *The Universe Has Your Back* by Gabby Bernstein, a protegée of Dr Dyer. The conclusion here is that whether we believe wisdom lies deep within us or arrives through a connection with the universal intelligence, we have within us pools of wisdom that are much deeper than we know, if we would only get out of our own way and listen:

> Today I surrender my goals and plans to the care of the Universe. I offer up my agenda and accept spiritual guidance. I trust that there is a plan far greater than mine. I know that where there once was lack and limitation there are spiritual solutions and creative ideas. I step back and let love lead the way. Thy will be done.

Remember, you can check out my favourite books and other resources for Exporting Crap, Importing Wisdom at www. healthywealthyandwiseuk.com/met.

5

FUEL UP FOR THE JOURNEY

When health is absent, wisdom cannot reveal itself,
art cannot manifest, strength cannot fight,
wealth becomes useless, and intelligence cannot be applied.

Herophilus

GOOD HEALTH IS NON-NEGOTIABLE FOR METAMORPHOSIS

If any of us were polled on our top priority in life, we'd probably answer: 'my health.' However, I suspect that on a day-to-day basis, many of us take our health for granted. I know I tend to do this. I once heard Oprah declare that first thing in the morning she practices gratitude for simply being able to swing her legs out of bed and pad across the bedroom to the bathroom. For the fortunate majority of us, this simple act is a given unless it's taken away. And when it's removed, as Herophilus noted above, everything else suffers.

The funny thing is that while most of us take it for granted that we are generally able-bodied and highly functioning, we conversely take it for granted that we feel slightly tired, fuzzy, stiff, forgetful, lethargic, and overall fairly crappy much of the time. We seem to exist in a twilight zone where we're 'basically fine' but not exactly full of vitality. We're blessed to be free from major disease or pain, but we're not exactly firing on all cylinders. When was the last time you described yourself as feeling vital? Thought not.

The other assumption that we make about our health is that we are on an inevitable, slow decline towards old age, with that decline manifesting as a gradual increase in the symptoms I mentioned above. We assume that we'll grow stiffer, more hunched-over, more forgetful, and less energetic as we age. We dread it – but we accept it as a given.

Let me tell you something: while these scenarios may be *common*, they are not *normal*, and they are certainly not inevitable. Whatever Big Pharma and the medical insurance industry would like you to believe, we can completely reinvigorate our overall wellbeing and our ageing process.

I mentioned in the introduction to this book that I had been exhausted, frazzled, and reactive with zero clarity. I had constant brain-fog. I felt hungover every morning, even when I hadn't drunk. My energy (and mood) swings were horrible. When I made the choice to wake up, reevaluate my life, and make it extraordinary, **my single biggest decision was to fix my health.** Doing so over the last few months has changed everything for me and it has given me the strength I needed to fix many other aspects of my life too.

I'm not a doctor or a nutritionist, but I'm here to tell you that if your health is sub-optimal and you feel constantly sluggish, you won't have much luck making lasting changes in life because it's *just too tiring*. We spoke before about the fact that just reacting to daily life takes up so much bandwidth. To find the energy to move beyond reacting to acting, our poor bodies need to be nurtured like a race-horse.

Now it's time for the good news. In this chapter we're going to cover:

- How so many of our chronic health problems often have the same underlying cause (and why traditional healthcare is ill-equipped to treat them),
- My story, which shows how quickly you can see and feel great results,
- Why proper knowledge of your body really is power,
- Some mental tricks and tips for making the right choices for your health,
- Why making this commitment to yourself is *amazing* and you'll never look back.

WHY TRADITIONAL MEDICINE STRUGGLES WITH ROOT CAUSES

If you break your arm or contract pneumonia, our western healthcare system is incredible. Acute conditions and trauma are their bag. However, the biggest burden on our healthcare systems is now chronic illness and specifically the Big Four (type II diabetes, Alzheimer's, cancer, and heart disease). With the establishment of vaccinations, antibiotics, and safety measures such as seatbelts, it's the Big Four that are likely to kill you or, at least, make your life miserable.

Below these killers lie a host of insidious chronic conditions that eat away at our wellbeing and quality of life. Migraines, sinus infections, rheumatoid arthritis, IBS, eczema, asthma, tonsillitis, and many others belong in this category. Here's the rub. Our doctors tend to be trained in silos so they treat these conditions in isolation, often without considering any other parts of our physiology (our doctors also receive close to no nutrition training in medical school, but let's not go there).

I've seen dermatologists, ENT specialists, and gastroenterologists for years, for seemingly unrelated conditions. The twist? They were all related. The spoiler? None of these professionals had any lasting success finding cures for my conditions, despite their steroids/ antibiotics/ antifungals/ offers of surgery.

Today we live in a society that our bodies weren't built for. We have not evolved biologically to handle pollution, chemical fertiliser, processed food, GMOs, and EMFs, not to mention constant, self-induced stress. These stressors play havoc with our genes, our cells, and our endocrine systems. They are headwinds for our vitality and wellbeing and they cause the majority of our physical dis-ease and deterioration.

While traditional medicine continues to be siloed by speciality, to largely ignore nutrition, and to focus on managing symptoms rather than preventing them, I fear that we'll continue to see chronic dis-ease build and make millions of us miserable. When I started to ask questions about my own health, I found many of the answers through functional medicine.

MY JOURNEY THROUGH FUNCTIONAL MEDICINE

I'm not convinced that reading about other people's health issues makes for much of a page-turner so I'll keep this focused on my learnings and on potential implications for *you*.

In short, after ten years on a trading floor followed by two children (with a 20-month gap between them) and entrepreneurship, I felt tired and sluggish most of the time. I was functioning as normally as many other people but I didn't accept that that was a good enough state in which to live. I had constant brain-fog and huge energy slumps. I couldn't last between meals without (often sugary) snacks. I had frequent blood sugar crashes which were aggressive enough to ensure that I always had snacks to hand in the car in case the crashes impacted my ability to drive safely.

I also had a whole host of other chronic problems. The main symptoms were regular sinus infections which were hard to treat without antibiotics, debilitating tension headaches, and ongoing bloating and stomach pains. For many of these symptoms, I had seen a whole host of doctors over the previous twenty years without any permanent resolution to my ailments.

The Functional Way

I started to learn about functional, or integrative, medicine through various blogs and podcasts and became fascinated by the premise that when our physiology is in homeostasis everything functions smoothly, but that various factors can throw this out of whack and cause widespread symptoms, or dis-ease. I love reframing 'disease' as 'dis-ease' because it implies that our bodies use our symptoms to send us messages of underlying problems, or root causes.

This is the heart of functional medicine. It is not woo-woo or airy fairy. On the contrary, it is highly empirical and utilises many detailed tests with which traditional doctors may be unfamiliar. It assesses all of the body's main processes (e.g. cellular communication, detoxification, defence) in a holistic fashion to understand where the body is compromised and what the root causes may be (whether food, environmental toxins, stress or others).

A prominent theme in functional medicine is that when you identify the root cause of a problem, you can often use that root cause to help to restore balance in that area. For many of us, food is a major driver of dis-ease. Therefore, we can often achieve amazing results by reducing or eliminating problematic food groups while increasing intake of beneficial foods and often introducing heavy supplement usage for a period to restore homeostasis.

What I found fascinating, was that whenever I discussed my chronic tiredness, apathy, and sub-optimal cognitive function with friends or business associates, people would look at me in amazement. 'What do you expect?' they would reply. 'You're running a business and you've got two kids. Of course you're tired!' When it comes to ill health or a lack of vitality, the widespread perception in our society is still to suck it up. Parenthood explains tiredness. Ageing explains mental and physical deterioration. We're told there's nothing to do about it. Well, I had read enough to know that that was a load of bollocks.

I found a wonderful functional practitioner in London. She is a GP who headed up a London hospital's diabetes unit before becoming disheartened by the traditional ways of treating diabetes (essentially, putting patients on insulin). We have been working together for over six months and she has transformed my health.

What Did We Find?

Well, we have assessed and treated several different areas over the last six months to avoid overwhelming my body at any one time. Over this period, we discovered that:

- My gut was, to put it bluntly, fairly screwed. My microbiome was inadequate and I had Candida, a yeast infection (from too much sugar and wheat!). *Treatment: targeted probiotics, cut down sugar.*
- My gut absorption was poor. I was eating lots of nutrients but they weren't being absorbed into the blood stream. *Treatment: amino acids.*
- My anti-nuclear antibodies (the antibodies that protect the nuclei of my cells) were elevated, suggesting the very early stages of an autoimmune condition. *Treatment: auto-immune protocol. Cut out gluten and all grains and dairy for three months. My antibody levels have now normalised.*
- I had various deficiencies and wasn't eating enough Omega-3 fatty acids, which are so essential for cognitive function (our brains are 60% fat). *Treatment: heavy supplement programme for three months.*
- I had several fairly unpleasant parasites in my gut. *Treatment: antibiotics and antifungal medication.*
- My thyroid was sluggish. Notably the driver was my T3 hormone (not my T4, which is the main hormone that regular doctors check). *Treatment: supplements to provide thyroid support. My thyroid*

function has now normalised and I now find it much easier to maintain my optimal body weight.

- I had a marked cortisol deficiency as well as deficiencies in some other hormones. It seemed I had quite literally used up all my stress hormones over twenty years of working on a trading floor, parenting small children, and running a business. *Treatment: prescriptions for some 'parent' hormones (my term) which my body can use to allocate to the pathways most in need. I have just started this course at the time of writing.*

Over the past six months I've made amazing strides and I feel like a different person. I bounce out of bed in the morning, I'm able to go longer without meals, and I haven't had a sinus infection or severe headache in six months. My brain-fog has cleared up and my cognitive function is much improved.

I'm particularly excited about being able to improve my hormonal reserves in a really thoughtful manner. Hormone depletion happens to both men and women and can play havoc with our quality of life. By taking these steps now and optimising my diet, I fully intend to pass through the menopause and into my later years with energy and vitality.

WHY KNOWLEDGE IS POWER WHERE OUR BODIES ARE CONCERNED

I know that I am not alone in having years of frustration, suffering, and confusion where my health is concerned. I also know that many people have suffered far more than me; by today's standards I've had a pretty pain-free existence. One thing I cannot stand is *not knowing* why symptoms flare up and why I feel just rubbish enough to make the daily grind that bit harder. I believe that knowledge is power and that the wealth of insight and understanding that I've accumulated about my amazing, resilient body is a complete game-changer.

We often treat our bodies harshly. We stuff them full of crappy processed food and don't give them enough rest. When they try to send us messages, we silence them with pharmaceuticals. As Dr Maya Shetreat says in her *amazing* book, *The Dirt Cure*:

> Chances are that you take much more than you give, whether you insist that your body keep up with your usual tasks when you're not feeling well or ask it to perform without the optimal fuel or rest. Your expectation of your body is likely high while your community with it is low.

For me, shifting from that mentality to one of listening to my body has been transformative. I've gone from wondering why my body is letting me down when I get ill, to taking on board its feedback and instead asking how *I* may be letting *it* down. We're on the same side and it feels great.

My hormone deficiencies have just come to light. When my doctor first met me, one of the first things she said was: 'I bet you have a cortisol deficit.' However, because hormones are one of the first things to regulate themselves with an improved diet and lifestyle, and to avoid treating everything at once and over-taxing my body (and bank-balance!) we have only begun to look at them.

Over the past few months, I've often berated myself for not being more resilient. I found the process of closing down my company emotionally exhausting and highly fraught. I frequently find parenthood to be the same! I often beat myself up for over-reacting to the kids' misdemeanours, especially around the 'witching hour' when I'm tired and hungry. But guess what? My hormone tests show that my cortisol levels go through the floor late in the afternoon. They are practically at zero, below the bottom of the 'normal' range. I quite literally have no stress resilience at that time of day. I have no reserves upon which to draw when I find myself in a trying situation. The tests have therefore been a revelation for me. They've replaced my negative internal chatter with a physiological picture which I am empowered to *change.*

I want to make one thing very clear. Almost every deficiency or problem that my doctor has identified has been *resolved.* It's required a huge amount of compliance and self-discipline (there we go again; I told you it's the key to everything!) on my part. Where I've been less disciplined, my progress has been slower (Candida, I'm looking at you). On the whole, I've been well rewarded for my efforts which has made this a very worthwhile exercise for me. The results I've seen in my health have dramatically improved my quality of life. I can't ever remember having had this much energy, clarity, and drive before. Across all the aspects of metamorphosis that I've outlined up until now, I doubt I would have been able to make the progress I have without investing in this incredible body that has yielded me two children and continues to be strong and resilient in the face of all that I throw at it.

Daily life is tough. Committing to metamorphosing and choosing to grow and spread our wings is tougher. We need to bring our bodies along for the journey.

WHERE SHOULD YOU START WITH FUNCTIONAL MEDICINE?

The first thing to be aware of is that seeing a functional practitioner, undergoing the necessary tests, and purchasing the supplements and private prescriptions is far from cheap. Each consultation will likely cost several hundred pounds or dollars, and most of the tests I had were at least £100 each. The first time I saw my doctor, I spent £750 on tests and £500 on supplements. It's a big financial commitment and therefore understandably out of reach for a very broad swathe of the population. That said, my husband and I made the decision to tighten our belts in other ways and make our health a budget (and lifestyle) priority. I also found that forking out so much money made me ultra-invested in ensuring that I religiously took my supplements and followed my new regime.

I'm well aware that undergoing this journey thoroughly and with a highly qualified professional is a major luxury, and I feel very fortunate and grateful to be in a position to do it. I've taken a pretty intense path to optimising my health. However, the good news is that there are so many resources out there to help you learn more about this approach and shed light on what your body's stressors may be through diagnostics. We live in an amazing age!

Today you can get many diagnostics done by post. You can run DNA tests by taking a mouth swab (I did this with DNAFit before meeting my doctor), hormone tests through companies such as DUTCH by peeing on five pieces of paper at different times of day, and you can even send off some poo and find out what intestinal parasites you have. FUN! Many of these companies do a great job of explaining the significance of the data to you, without needing a functional practitioner. DNAFit included a thirty-minute phone consultation with a nutritionist to optimise my diet to fit my genes. DUTCH provides lots of diagrams to illustrate your hormonal state and also offers more detailed explanatory videos online.

The way in which a functional practitioner adds value is by acting as a detective, piecing together a vast array of both quantitative and anecdotal data to build a picture of your lifestyle and to understand *why* various malfunctions or symptoms may be occurring and *how* to treat them. It's an extremely nuanced, sophisticated practice.

One example: are my sugar cravings the result of a yeast infection or of insulin resistance? Another example: my Omega-3 deficiency could be treated with simple Omega-3 capsules but my doctor identified the fact that I was far more deficient in DHA than EPA and prescribed supplements accordingly. If the treatment we receive at the hands of our harassed, over-worked NHS GPs may sometimes resemble painting by numbers, functional medicine is more akin to fine art.

Having said that, if you are generally healthy and looking to optimise rather than overhaul your health, you can make huge strides by reading around the subject and making some basic changes to your diet and lifestyle depending on your symptoms and situation. This is a fast-changing area and so I've opted to make most of the resources for this chapter available online at www.healthy-wealthyandwise.com/met-book-bonus but there are two books by functional practitioners (who are also medical doctors) that I particularly recommend:

The Disease Delusion by Dr Jeffrey Bland. This is an incredible book structured around the body's seven physiological processes. Each section contains plenty of questions to help you self-diagnose if you suspect you have health problems in that particular area, and there is a lengthy questionnaire at the end.

The Inflammation Spectrum by Dr Will Cole. Dr Cole specialises in auto-immune diseases and the book discusses the ways in which excessive or chronic inflammation can affect us in a myriad of ways. It features a questionnaire and suggests some temporary elimination diets to help you unearth the culprits affecting your wellbeing.

In conclusion, if you have or are genetically at risk of a disease that can be seen as metabolic (cancer, type II diabetes, Alzheimer's, or heart disease) or you suffer from an auto-immune disease (or suspect that you do), then I believe functional medicine is a great way to go. One final word of warning: many of these conditions can slowly build over ten to twenty years before the symptoms become marked enough to warrant a formal diagnosis, so it's never too early to start making small, preventative tweaks that could have big results over many years.

MENTAL TIPS AND HACKS TO DRIVE HEALTHY CHOICES

Even if we know what is and is not good for our health, executing on that knowledge can be painful. Believe me, I know! However, our minds can be pliable creatures. Here are a few tips to win the mindset battle.

Knowledge is also Willpower

Here's what I found. The more knowledge I have about exactly what is going on in my body, the more I'm able to harness my willpower to make the right choices. My reasoning: it removes all the trial and error so I believe that the actions I take will have targeted, effective results.

If I didn't know what was causing my symptoms or suboptimal test results, then I'd likely have to try lots of different things to see which ones helped, which quite frankly is painful and dull. I don't want to have exclude every food type under the sun one-by-one. The feedback that the tests have given me is very clear, as are the steps I need to take to improve my results. If I know that taking GTA and Thyrostim (the latter is hideous to swallow and makes me gag every time) will improve my thyroid function, then that's a sacrifice I'm willing to make. I trust that my doctor has made my entire regimen as efficient as possible which means that I know I'm not wasting time and energy faffing around with unnecessary drugs or dietary exclusions. This knowledge improves my willpower.

Create a Positive Feedback Loop

If the regime is efficient and effective then you may see results quite quickly. My improvements have been sufficiently consistent and marked to encourage me to stay on my path. I see my doctor every three months, so I'm not getting constant feedback, but when she runs the next set of tests and I find that many of my biomarkers have significantly normalised, I am thrilled.

If you are committed to making some lifestyle changes for the good of your health, I'd suggest a weekly journaling practice to check in on your main symptoms or pain-points (figuratively and literally). I actually didn't notice how much my brain-fog had cleared up until my doctor asked me how it was. By bringing regular consciousness to the messages your body is or is not telling you, you will likely create a feedback loop for yourself and my hope is that your physical progress (whether it's weight-loss, reduction of headaches etc.) provides the boost you need to keep on track.

Your Why: The Carrot and the Stick

It's well-documented that when we have a strong sense of purpose, we are more driven and more committed to our cause. I did the following exercise as a part of Lifebook Online, a course run by Mindvalley and created by Jon and Missy Butcher. As an aside, the Butchers are fifty-something grandparents who are insanely wealthy, look incredible, and have a beautiful, well-rounded, 'twelve-category strong' (their words) life which they created using their Lifebook framework.

The first category that we addressed in Lifebook Online was Health and Fitness. After setting our vision for our health, Jon asked us to define our purpose for wanting to excel in this category. He likened it to the carrot-and-stick approach: how would it feel if I won this battle, and *what pain would it cause me to lose;* what was I *not* willing to endure in the future?

This approach was a real lightbulb moment for me and I found the process emotional. Here are the *Whys* I listed:

How would it feel if I won this battle?

- Having a huge amount of energy for my family
- Having a huge amount of brainpower to devote

to career and personal development - because I have big goals
- Less joint ache and discomfort
- No sinus infections
- Feeling gorgeous and radiant
- Needing less sleep
- Mental clarity
- No sugar/ energy dips
- Living longer, with no pain
- Enjoying many more decades of a vital, full life – with incredible life experiences
- Looking and feeling as young as I can for as long as I can

Now, what pain will it cause me if I don't achieve my vision? What am I *not* willing to experience?

- Lack of energy to enjoy my kids
- Lack of energy to do well in my career
- Feeling unrefreshed when I wake up in the morning
- Brain-fog leading to Alzheimer's or dementia
- Getting cancer
- The fear of getting sick in the future or current ailments getting worse
- Ageing or deteriorating more quickly than I need to
- Spending *any* time in hospital

The power here lies in being able to see the big picture. By identifying healthy behaviour with the most important parts of my vision for my health, and identifying unhealthy behaviour with the experiences that I am simply not willing to endure if I can possibly help it, I find that I have a powerful *framework* that acts like horses' blinkers, to keep me squarely on track.

What's Your Framework?

Above, I mentioned a philosophical framework which keeps me focused on my biggest goal – to optimise my health. It's also helpful to have frameworks for *execution.* One of my favourites comes from *The Code of the Extraordinary Mind.* Lakhiani is a computer scientist and likes to codify things. He suggests thinking of our perception of the world, or our 'models of reality', as our hardware. Then, we can consider everything that we do – our routines, habits and behaviours – as our 'systems for living', or our software.

The great thing about software is that it can be updated regularly. I find this analogy very helpful for the arena of my health and fitness. The key message is that it's ok, encouraged even, to swap out better routines and systems for tired ones whenever we find them. If you decide you prefer yoga to Pilates, or keto to paleo, then swap them out! Science moves fast and I like to try to keep up. We know by now that nothing is sacred and that scientific progress can overturn theories that were previously considered as fact.

For this very reason, I've opted to keep many of the resources for this chapter out of the book itself. I'm committed to updating these regularly online and you can find a full list of experts, podcasts, and reading lists on www. healthywealthyandwiseuk.com/met.

6

FAREWELL TO LIMITING BELIEFS, WELCOME TO LIMITLESS LIVING

After all, if you loved yourself truly and deeply, would you limit your life to what you previously thought possible? Nope. You'd blow your own socks off.

Kamal Ravikant

So here we are! This is the final step in the metamorphosis process. Before we shatter the cocoon for good, let's take stock of how far we've come. Over the last five chapters we have:

- actively chosen to live life in the ten faces of consciousness and to get curious about our habitual behaviours and reactions
- acknowledged that taking 100% responsibility for everything in our lives by accepting and owning our circumstances is true empowerment
- embraced self-discipline as the key to absolutely

everything, defined our motivations to turbo-charge our willpower, and committed to forging new habits
- invested in our brains by upgrading the content that we allow into them and by tapping into the wisdom that lies within us
- clarified why this extraordinary journey requires extraordinary health and learnt how we can truly empower ourselves to optimise our wellbeing.

SPOILER: WE ARE ALREADY LIMITLESS

The ultimate secret of a life well-lived is that we are already limitless – we are already butterflies. The ultimate tragedy is that most of us are unaware of that. To be limitless, we need to release ourselves from the shackles. You know, the ones that we put on ourselves, the ones that aren't actually locked? This chapter will show you how to break free from our self-imposed prisons and FLY.

WHAT ARE LIMITING BELIEFS?

Recently, I was helping my son Paddy with his English homework. He had been given ten sentences and his task was to identify each one as fact or opinion, marking with them a nice clear F or O.

For Paddy, the job was fairly straightforward. The little man gamely and successfully separated out the facts from the opinions. I couldn't help but be amused by this. If only the difference between the two was so clearly marked in real life!

Limited beliefs are toxic, insidious phenomena whose very menace lies in the simple fact that *most of the time, we are unaware that we have them.* There are very few absolute truths in life, far fewer than I, as a liberal from a western culture, would like to believe exist. There are far more relative truths and there are a zillion limiting beliefs that underpin the existence of every one of us on any given day.

Limiting beliefs are otherwise known as false perceptions, internal narratives, the stories we tell ourselves, the ladder of inference, or the 'meaning-making machine' inside our head. Essentially, they are a malfunction of the perfectly understandable frameworks we create in our head to make sense of this complex, crazy world. They are our perceptions, turned into monsters.

We can have limiting beliefs about anything and everything. Examples include:

- My parents are [insert name of organised religion] so I have to be that way too.
- I could never run a marathon/ write a book/ set up my own business/ try public speaking.
- Good girls don't ask for too much.
- Money is the root of all evil.
- I'm chubby/ bitchy/ bad at tennis – *that's just the way I am.*
- I'm not worthy of being happy/ rich/ loved/ married [or insert any other blessing].
- I am not enough.

Vishen Lakhiani talks a lot about limiting beliefs in *The Code of the Extraordinary Mind*. He says:

 Human beings are far less rational than we think. Many ideas we hold dear and cling to as 'truth' fall apart under close inspection.

Lakhiani calls the false perspectives that we hold about our world 'Brules' – bullshit rules 'that we adopt to simplify our understanding of the world'. It's entirely understandable that we have adopted these rules. We form many of them at a very young age, which is why so many of us spend adulthood working through our 'issues' – decades of baggage that we acquired as children and drag around as adults, weighing us down.

Of course, we can't work on our limiting beliefs until we become aware of them. If you look again at the list above, you may identify with some but you may also notice that you take these as fact; you have internalised them. A good example is my own health. In the last chapter, I discussed my quest for optimal health. However, before I became aware of functional medicine, I had taken many of my symptoms to be 'just who I am.' I've always been congested. I've always suffered from bloating. Therefore, that must be just the way I was made, right? WRONG. The symptoms that I'd seen as an absolute truth were cries for help from a body out of sync. The scary thing is how easy it is for us to *accept* a multitude of things about our health, our relationships, our capabilities, and the pressures of our culture without ever questioning them. That stops now.

Our Perceptions Can Be a Great Source of Pain for Us and Our Relationships

The tragedy of the limits we place on ourselves is clear when we look at the list above. How many of us are doomed to die believing that we're not enough, or regretting that we could never find the courage to overcome our self-imposed limits?

But here's the other thing. There are billions of us, all

with our entirely unique perspective on how the world works. Surely, an enormous proportion of those perspectives must be at odds with each other? Of course they are. This is the concept of Us and Them. It's why we've had centuries of religious wars and terrorism. It's why families in the UK were torn apart by the Brexit vote. It's also why we clash with each other so often.

So much of the upset in our human relationships comes from the fact that we have different rules from each other. When someone else unwittingly breaks one of our rules, we can start clambering up that ladder of inference *immediately*. For example, I love birthdays. A rule that I have unconsciously created is that when you love someone, you must make a fuss of them on their birthday. It follows that I would perceive a lack of fuss as a lack of love.

My husband, however, could not give a toss about his own birthday and therefore sees no reason to go all out for anyone else's. We've had to have a frank conversation about my expectations on this front. It's important to me that he knows that my birthday means a lot to me. Conversely, it's really crucial for me to understand that any lack of exuberance on his part around my birthday does *not* signify a lack of affection for me.

We humans are funny creatures; we cannot begin to know what is in each other's heads. I've concluded that the best thing we can do is to question our own motives when we can, while taking care not to make assumptions about other people's motives. This, however, is easier said than done ...

IF THEY'RE BLIND SPOTS, HOW ARE WE SUPPOSED TO SEE THEM?!

My coach, Charlotte, is also a very dear friend. I had never experienced coaching before working with her, and I was sceptical of what benefits it would give me. In actuality, I had a lightbulb moment every single session. The leaps I made were extraordinary. Charlotte's secret? She is a highly skilled coach, and it helps that she has known me for two decades. But her main advantage? *She is not me.*

Have you ever noticed how easy it is to give advice to a friend? The issues that most perplex and torment our friends are often crystal-clear to us. Blind spots are only blind spots for ourselves.

In one of my sessions with Charlotte, we were addressing my mental block around selling. I don't like selling, and at this time I was convinced that I wasn't any good at it (tricky given I was running an e-commerce fashion brand). I'm not alone. For homework, Charlotte asked me to read Dan Pink's *To Sell Is Human*, and in it he confirms that when people are asked to identify phrases relating to the term 'selling', they think of words like 'sleazy' or 'used-car salesman', etc.

In this case, my horror of selling was getting in the way of my ability to drive my business forward. Then Charlotte leaned forward and said, 'But Sara! I have bought every single book you've ever recommended to me! You're an amazing saleswoman!'

This was my lightbulb moment. I had consistently told myself that I neither liked nor was skilled at selling. What I realised is that, because I am naturally highly enthusiastic, I tend to do a great job of making that enthusiasm infectious. When I wax lyrical about the life-changing powers of a good book, my friends feel inspired and compelled to buy said book.

It turns out that my real passion is selling and communicating *ideas* rather than product, and that is one of the reasons that I find myself turning to writing. We'll discuss this more in Chapter 9: 'What Do We Actually Want from Life?' The point I want to make here is that the story I had told myself, the limiting belief that I had taken as gospel, in no way reflected my reality as Charlotte and other people in my life saw it. These days, I make a conscious effort not to make assumptions about what I am and am not capable of. Why box myself in?

Import and Download Wisdom to Bring your Blind Spots to Light

There are several ways we can seek to uncover these blind spots, these unconscious (but deadly) limiting beliefs.

Get a Coach or a Therapist

Professionals like Charlotte are trained to identify our blind spots. One of the reasons that they can achieve great success with their clients is that they awaken us to our blind spots; in a way, they're saving us from ourselves. Of course, there as many forms of professionals available to us as there are blind spots. Also, the differences between coaches and therapists are significant and it's important to identify the right professional for your particular needs, whether you are struggling with past trauma or endeavouring to fulfil the future of your dreams. Nevertheless, working with someone who can help you to unlock yourself can be hugely rewarding.

Ask Your Friends, Family, Co-workers: Anyone Who Knows You Well

Here's a cheaper solution. At the very end of *The Miracle Morning*, Hal Elrod shared with his readers an exercise that changed his life. It consisted of nothing more complicated than sending an email to a couple of dozen friends and family members asking them to give him their utterly honest opinion of him, and being entirely receptive to the feedback that he got, using it to shape his growth objectives. He found the courage to do this because he recognised that he could never get a full picture of himself without their input, and it proved an incredible way for him to accelerate his personal growth.

I don't know about you, but just reading about this makes me want to hide under my bed and cover my eyes. It is horrifying! I have always struggled with being able to accept any kind of constructive feedback without shrivelling up into a ball. It's been a long-time limitation and I'm working on it, but I'm not sure I'm ready for Elrod's exercise just yet.

Billionaire hedge fund manager, Ray Dalio, also has a crowd-sourcing technique to overcome his blind spots and limitations. In his book, *Principles*, he discusses the practice of 'radical transparency' espoused by his hedge fund, Bridgewater Associates. At Bridgewater, all staff members are encouraged to challenge the ideas of any of the investment team, even Dalio himself. For Dalio, this is a no-brainer. As he explains in the book, any dent to his ego is absolutely worth it if it means that he makes the right investment choice. He says:

I just want to be right – I don't care if the right
answer comes from me.

It's hard to argue with that logic.

Play Devil's Advocate. Question Everything.

One of the best ways to shed light on our unconscious assumptions is to question what we're doing and how we're reacting. In Chapter 1 we looked at the boost to consciousness that getting curious can have. When we give ourselves permission to question everything, it means that no assumptions are sacred.

On a recent business course, I attended a lecture on innovation. The professor focused much of the session on how to uncover blind spots. He proposed the acronym AOI: Assumption, Opposite, Implement. We can benefit from taking our beliefs, temporarily assuming that the complete opposite is true, and implementing new practices based on this premise.

Tim Ferriss takes a similar approach in *Tools of Titans*. He offers a list of questions we can ask ourselves when we feel stuck, one of which is 'What if I did the opposite for 48 hours?'

Let's take my approach to maths as an example. I've always considered myself to be poor at maths. When I was fifteen, my maths teacher told my parents: 'It doesn't come naturally to her.' Inevitably, I felt compelled to prove him wrong and gained an A* grade in my maths GCSE. I've never been so proud of an academic achievement!

Nevertheless, my anxiety around maths has continued to plague me. When I was a banker, I lived in fear that my very sketchy understanding of more sophisticated products such as convertible bonds would be exposed. When I was an entrepreneur, I dreaded the scenario of an investor firing questions at me about my EBITDA projections (Earnings before Interest, Tax, Depreciation, and Amortisation, in case you were wondering). Even the thought of it made me break out into a cold sweat.

In short, I have a limiting belief around maths. In fact, I may suffer from Mathematics Anxiety (yes, it's a thing). How could I benefit from using the AOI framework?

I could look for evidence to disprove my theory: my grades at school and the fact that I thrived as a banker for ten years and a business-owner for eight.

I could embrace a growth mindset: I am fully capable of improving my maths ability if I choose to, by committing to more learning and testing around this subject.

I could change another part of the narrative I tell myself: Maths is not my strongest skill-set but *that's okay.* My maths skills are sufficient for my needs; I can outsource problematic areas such as book-keeping to professionals and focus my time on my areas of strength. By doing this, I've shown the self-awareness that allows me to understand my strengths and weaknesses, but I have not allowed my weaknesses to define me or to limit my goals.

Questions are such a powerful way to get unstuck. If you think about it, they are a therapist's main asset. When we frame an issue as a question, it alerts our brains to the possibility that this issue may not be grounded in fact. In *The Code of the Extraordinary Mind*, Lakhiani suggests two questions that can help us to re-write our models of reality. They are:

 Is my model of reality absolute or relative truth?

Does this really mean what I think it means?

I find the first question valuable both for challenging cultural norms and when I am struggling to ascertain whether something is fact or circumstance. Is it immutable or can it be changed? I am five foot six. Fact. I am 'always' bloated. Circumstance. I can change this condition; I should not accept it as a necessary evil. A useful sanity check is to ask *what* I am assuming and *why*.

The second question is used to sanity-check our reactions. Lakhiani references Morty and Shelly Lefkoe who have done extensive research on our 'meaning-making machines.' They suggest that we can manufacture up to 500 meanings per week. Instead, by asking ourselves the question:

 Is this really true? Am I 100 percent sure that this is what's really going on?

We can reduce these dramatically.

WHAT HAPPENS WHEN WE SHED OUR LIMITING BELIEFS?

When we start to shed these beliefs, we become boundless. Our perceptions dictate our reality. Remember the four-minute mile? As soon as Roger Bannister demonstrated that the four-minute limitation was nothing more than an artificial construct, his rival found the strength to beat his record in 46 days. To revert to my opening words for this chapter, we are limitless. We set our own limitations. We are in a prison of our own making.

Successful people understand that they cannot achieve their goals by operating within society's perceived boundaries. In *Miracle Morning Millionaires,* David Osborn writes:

Effective self-leaders closely examine their beliefs, decide which ones serve them, and eliminate those that don't. When you find yourself stating anything that sounds like a limiting belief, from 'I don't have enough time' to 'I could never do that,' pause and turn your self-limiting statements into empowering questions, such as the following: Where can I find more time in my schedule? How might I be able to do that?

In other words, by questioning everything and refusing to take no for an answer, we open ourselves up to possibilities that may have seemed closed to us. This is a growth mindset, and I'm thrilled that it's core to the learning philosophy at my children's wonderful school. In my view, we can't learn this early enough.

WELCOME TO LIMITLESS LIVING

We're almost at the end of the metamorphosis process itself. The cocoon hangs open and we teeter on the precipice of a magical life. Before we spread our wings and take flight, we will need to draw some strength for the journey ahead. This strength comes from following a beautiful, simple philosophy:

Just be yourself.

In fact, just be.

We are supposed to know how to 'just be.' We are supposed to be human *beings*. We have traded this in to become human *doings*.

I listened to an interview with high performance

psychologist, Dr Michael Gervais, on the Goop podcast. He observed:

 Many of us think that to BE extraordinary we need to DO extraordinary – with this comes fatigue and anxiety. The best in the world are now focusing on BEING – creative, present, happy, and letting the mastery flow from that.

There are so many tragedies in our circumstances. We've discussed the tragedy of our self-imposed limitations. Another tragedy is our need to identify with our actions and achievements, the need to be busy and to over-extend ourselves.

JUST BE YOURSELF

We are not our achievements. We are not our bodies, our possessions, our jobs, or even our names. We just *are.*

Deepak Chopra employs a powerful practice to bring this home. Take a look at how it plays out for me.

I am Sara Madderson, an author from London.

I am Sara Madderson, an author.

I am Sara Madderson.

I am Sara.

I am.

I am.

We over-associate with the trappings of our circumstances and our environment. I certainly do this. It's why we suffer identity crises when we get fired, when we get divorced, when our children flee the nest. Without these anchors we don't know who we are. But if you repeat the exercise above you may find that it's curiously liberating to leave those anchors. What a relief it feels to just *be*. How exhausting it is to do anything else.

Let's turn back to the phrase *I am*.

The late Dr Wayne Dyer believed that *I am* is one of the most powerful statements available to us and he wrote copiously on this subject in his latter years. In one of his final books, *Wishes Fulfilled*, he notes that God and Jesus use *I am* with great frequency in the Bible. The words *I am* also give enormous currency to what follows them. Given their potency, Dyer cautions against cutting off our own power at the source by misusing them. The three ways to misuse them are by stating:

1. I am *not*.

2. I am [insert something negative: unworthy, exhausted, scared].

3. I *will be* (which is another way of saying that you are not yet).

He says:

 Notice how those around you, particularly family and close friends, use and misuse the inherent power of I am in their lives. Observe that many people say, 'I am weak, poor, depressed, sick, sad, afraid, unlucky and so on, and they continue to attract that into their life.

The Power of I Am Affirmations

We can use the power of *I am* whenever we want. I am a relatively recent convert to the magic of affirmations. I confess I used to find them fairly cringeworthy. But I've been employing them as part of my Miracle Morning™ practice, and I find the simple action of repeating them aloud to be galvanising: they ground me, they inspire me, and they ensure that I start my day with my goals and ambitions squarely in front of me. Essentially, they help me to set the tone for my day.

You can use *I am* affirmations to:

- **remind** you of blessings that you may tend to take for granted (I am healthy, I am happy, I am loved, I am pain-free)
- **reframe** areas where your ego likes to worry and taunt you (I am abundant, I am successful, I am prosperous)
- **embody** powerful nouns and therefore more closely identify with these states (I am love, I am peace, I am light, I am joy)
- **manifest** future outcomes by stating them as already achieved (I am a mother, I am a best-selling author).

HOW LIMITLESS LIVING FEELS

It Feels Like a Life-Long Love-Affair With Yourself

Several times throughout the process of writing *Metamorphosis*, I've questioned myself. Am I right to be extolling the virtues of personal transformation? Is driving myself onwards the kindest way to be with myself, or it is a fatal flaw, born of a perfectionist character? If the latter, am I being irresponsible by urging others to take the same path as me? Should I just take a chill pill, stop for a breather, and enjoy my life and my kids? Do I have everything upside-down?

Then I come back to the wonderful quote by Kamal Ravikant at the start of this chapter. Here it is again for ease:

> After all, if you loved yourself truly and deeply, would you limit your life to what you previously thought possible? Nope. You'd blow your own socks off.

So there we have it. I am fully, marvellously committed to blowing my own socks off. I simply can't imagine another way to live.

The context of this quote is important. It's from Ravikant's short and startlingly beautiful book, *Love Yourself Like Your Life Depends On It*. After what he describes as an ego-driven boom and bust cycle, his investment blows up and he has a total breakdown. The only thing that helps? A mantra that comes to him one particularly bleak morning and grows stronger: *I love myself; I love myself; I love myself.*

I mentioned that I was raised Catholic. We were taught in school that we must love God above everyone else, even our parents. I remember being utterly unable to do this and feeling a terrible guilt that I had failed. I raise this because in that context, I'm pretty sure loving *ourselves* never even came into the equation. 'She loves herself' was only used as an insult, describing someone who was completely up their own arse. It always felt to me that self-love was a shameful construct of the ego rather than something to nurture.

When you don't love yourself, you are without your own best friend. I was fortunate enough, while running my fashion brand, to attend an event with the legendary Diane Von Furstenberg. She told us that whenever she walks through her front door, she smiles and winks at herself in the hallway mirror and says, 'Hi honey! I'm home!'

Von Furstenberg went on to say that our greatest relationship must always be with ourselves. It is easy to become used to the voice inside our heads. I know that I have said many things to myself that I would never dream of saying to a dear friend. What is friendship? It's love, support, understanding, respect, and, above all, *compassion*. When we love ourselves, we always have this dear friend in our corner. We become our own greatest cheerleader.

When I say that being limitless and loving ourselves are the same, I am deadly serious. We cannot be free to soar while there is a cruel, judgemental voice from which we can't escape. One of the most moving books I've read was *Dying to Be Me* by Anita Moorjani, who has become well-known for her NDE (near-death experience) after a long battle with cancer. While Moorjani's rapid and complete recovery was quite literally miraculous, so too was her transformation from someone who feared everything in life and had no sense of her own worth, to a woman who was utterly free.

The great lesson that Moorjani received while briefly on the other side was that there is unconditional love from the universe for us all. We don't have to prove ourselves; we are worthy of receiving it simply by virtue of our existence. She says:

 I now live my life from joy and not from fear ... Before, without even realising it, everything I did was to avoid pain or to please other people ... Since my NDE, I don't feel that I came back to *accomplish* anything. I only came back to *be*. Because of this, everything I do comes from love.

I find this very liberating. When Moorjani looked death in the face and found that it looked far more enticing than the half-life she'd been living, she lost her fear of death and pretty much everything else. I've adapted the first line from the quote above for my morning affirmations, and I now say daily: 'I live my life from joy and love and not from fear.' I believe that loving ourselves is one of the most transformative steps that we can take. Like any other relationship, it needs work, commitment, and patience. My plea to you is to make that commitment to yourself.

It Feels Like Unshakeable Self-Belief

When we are limitless we are free and unconstrained. One of the biggest shackles we put on ourselves is the fear of what others think. It follows that when we begin to love ourselves, we no longer need the high opinion of others to thrive. Neither do we require their belief that we can succeed. To reference Ravikant, we know that we can blow our own socks off.

Relying on the validation of others is a dangerous practice. A former boss once gave me what I still think is great advice: when someone offers you their opinion, 'apply the appropriate discount.' In other words, if they're a jack-ass, prone to jealousy, or downright mean, feel free to discount what they've said to you by a very wide margin. Conversely, if someone you genuinely love or respect criticises you, you should probably consider what they have to say.

While I think this is a pretty good rule of thumb for regular life, if we want to transform, we must learn to be immune to both the bad *and* good opinions of both bad *and* good people. While I know this to be true, I find it really, really difficult to practice. For example, I care deeply about what my husband thinks. He is my favourite person on the planet and a man of great integrity. I bask in his love and I bask in his praise.

The reason it's dangerous to rely on such praise is that I'm seeking external validation. My husband is not me, therefore he is external to me. Should he change his opinion of me, file for divorce, or die, I am far more compromised because the person who dictated my feelings of self-worth is gone.

I look at my children and notice how often they seek validation. When they've painted a beautiful picture at school they can't wait to share it with me and to revel in my inevitable gushing (because naturally, they are the most talented and perfect children in the world). Of course I'll keep praising them. Of course I'll keep telling them they are magical and unique and capable of achievements beyond their wildest dreams. But I won't do it to hook them on my praise and validation. I'll do it to stoke that flame of self-love and self-belief so that one day my words will be nice rather than necessary.

We all require human interaction and intimacy. I believe that's because we are all connected in this universe. When we are limitless, we still thrive on these connections but they don't validate us. Neither do they drive our goals and ambitions. When we have unshakeable self-belief, we set and pursue our own goals for the sheer joy of learning and growing.

It Feels Easy

My fashion company ultimately failed, from a financial perspective at least. I dislike the word *failure*, which we'll come back to later. But if you asked me why it failed, I would probably give you a list of practical reasons. It couldn't scale, the margins were too low, the retail industry was exceptionally harsh, discounting had become a vicious cycle on the high street, etc.

However, if you asked me for a more philosophical perspective, I would confess that I suspect *I tried too hard.* I wanted it too badly. I had such huge dreams, but many of them came from a place of ego. I wanted to make certain amounts in revenue and to dress certain A-list celebrities. I spent eight years striving with every ounce of energy to control outcomes. I learnt two things. Trying to control outcomes is exhausting. And it doesn't work.

I've always been a self-labelled control freak. I had a plan. I knew what I wanted. I assumed I could realise the outcome I wanted. It didn't happen. The irony is that I had a great eight years running my brand, and it would have been even more fun if I'd relaxed and enjoyed the ride. In any case, as things were falling apart within the company this summer, I decided it would be advisable for me to invest time in the thing I find most difficult in the world: *surrendering.*

It turns out that surrendering is a lot of fun! I found it surprisingly easy. I suspect this was due to the struggles I'd had as the business took a turn for the worse. I was so exhausted from pushing, pushing, pushing to make things happen that I got sick of straining and I leaned into the process. I surrendered to surrender.

Ever noticed how much more effective you are at stretching out your limbs after a really tough workout? You're too tired to resist. Instead, you embrace the stretch. This is how my surrender happened. If I'm right, then it's another tragic irony of life. We exhaust ourselves by pushing when we could have achieved our outcome by *allowing*. I've thought a lot about the fable of the wind and the sun competing to see who can get a man to remove his coat. Being the wind is a fairly shitty existence. I choose to be the sun.

I, of course, read my way into surrender. I had heard the advice a million times before but not absorbed it. Surrender. Let go of the outcome. Stop wanting things so badly. Be in a state of not grasping but not pushing away. Finally, something clicked in my tired soul and I heard the lesson properly: life is so much easier when you just allow it to be.

I credit Gabby Bernstein with much of my shift. I'd read *The Universe Has Your Back* over the summer and it really spoke to me. I mean, even the title is one of the most reassuring titles of all time! I then devoured her latest book (at the time of writing this), *Super Attractor*, and found its central message to be profound: we attract what we want in life by feeling good and allowing. Bernstein calls people like me 'pushers'.

 'Pushers have a fear-based belief that if they're not super productive, nothing will happen for them. Little do they know that their pushy energy is blocking their capacity to attract! The Universe doesn't respond as well to frantic energy.

Honestly Gabby, where were you eight years ago when I launched my business? I needed this!

We are limitless when life feels easy. Life feels easy when we are limitless. It's a virtuous circle. When we can relax, adopt some perspective, understand that life is short and we shouldn't sweat the small stuff, we aren't constrained by the petty fears and resentments that rule us. We recognise that we ourselves manufacture so much of life's stress and conflict and we simply choose not to engage. As Bernstein says,

 We must accept that good things can come easily.

We over-complicate so much in life, and yet the formula for limitless living is elegant in its simplicity. Love yourself. Believe in yourself. Enjoy the ride. Get out of your own way and *allow*.

This is what gives us wings.

My friends, it's time to spread those wings and fly.

Remember, you can check out my favourite books and other resources for
Farewell to Limiting Beliefs, Welcome to Limitless Living
at www.healthywealthyandwiseuk.com/met.

PART II

SPREAD YOUR WINGS AND FLY

7

PERCEPTION IS REALITY

*The world as we have created it is a process of our thinking. It
cannot be changed without changing our thinking.*

Albert Einstein

We can't *see* differently until we *are* different. This is the
most compelling reason to undertake a metamorphosis: it
empowers us to transform our perception of our world. It's
likely that your perceptions, and therefore your reality, have
altered since you started reading this book. Do you feel a
shift?

As you've become more conscious, you may have started
to see your daily reality differently, to gravitate away from
the faces of unconsciousness, to catch yourself on autopilot,
and to get curious about the way you react to triggers
instead of letting those reactions go unnoticed. You may feel
more awake and more alive. You may see more wonder in

the world and you may be adding new pieces to the glorious puzzle that is self-awareness.

As you've begun to take full responsibility, perhaps some truths have surfaced. They may be uncomfortable; it's uncomfortable to take ownership instead of deflecting blame. They may also be empowering; you may feel liberated by the realisation that you are in the driving seat of your own life, and so you may feel ready to lean into the necessary discomfort to reap the rewards on the other side.

As you start to flex your self-discipline muscle, you may feel the warm glow of making positive choices. You may be exploring your motivations and upgrading them to create powerful drivers for new habits, habits that may seem small but will cause great changes thanks to the compounding effect.

As you clear your mind of stressors, noise, inane reality TV, and other crap, it's my hope that you're enjoying some newfound head space. You may find that this brings you more peace and clarity. You may be exploring new content that offers new perspectives, wisdom, and opportunities for education.

As you revaluate your health and make it a non-negotiable part of your metamorphosis, you may be finding it easier to flex that self-discipline muscle and make some lifestyle changes. What once seemed like hard work and self-sacrifice, has perhaps become an investment into your future, made willingly and aligned with your long-term objectives for your health and vitality.

And finally, you may have already started to stare some of your limiting beliefs in the face. If you haven't quite thrown them all out yet, at least you have taken the first steps by shining a light on them and knowing that they are not hard, immutable facts, but nothing more than narratives that can be unwritten in favour of new narratives that will serve you on your journey.

If any of these suggestions are true, then consider what you've already achieved. You've altered your perception of your own reality, without any part of your external world having really changed at all. What have your friends, family members, and colleagues been doing while you've been metamorphosing? They've been doing *exactly what they've always done.* That may involve moaning, reacting, abdicating responsibility, blaming circumstance for their lack of promotion, treating every day like Groundhog Day, or watching too much *Love Island.* It's likely that your home, car, job, or bank balance hasn't changed much either (yet). You do not necessarily have to change your world; you just have to change how you view it. To return to Dr Dyer:

Change the way you look at things, and the things you look at change.

UPGRADING OUR PERCEPTIONS

This is a pivotal point in the process of metamorphosis. You've done so much already. You've looked inward and evaluated what you've found. You've made changes to your emotions, reactions, and behaviour. You've shaken off your cocoon and exchanged comfort and familiarity for the marvellous opportunities that await. You've done the hard work and now you are understandably ready to reap the rewards, to take flight, and soar to new heights of potential. But wait! Please give me a few more pages before you do.

When I told my family about my plans to write this book, my lovely mother looked at me with great sadness and said: 'But honey, I never knew you wanted to change your life!' That made me feel wretched, and I want to make clear to my mother and to you that I don't want to change my life. I have a beautiful life; it's charmed in every way. I'm so grateful for my blessings. I intend to fulfil my potential to the best of my ability, and I intend to live a life of happiness, purpose, and vitality.

A critical part of achieving this is upgrading my perceptions of life. We know that beauty is in the eye of the beholder. While we pause, poised for flight, this is the perfect moment to cast an eye over our life and recognise where the beauty lies. Now is the time to acknowledge how far we've come, how rich our blessings are, and how abundant our lives are already. It would be a tragedy if we used these hard-won wings to fly off to pastures greener, unaware of just how verdant the grass already is on our side of the fence.

We're therefore going to spend the next two chapters upgrading our perceptions of our current reality before we begin to use our newfound skills to go about improving it.

The Master Key

I find it helps to have an over-arching mantra or viewpoint on life, a hook on which we can hang all of our beliefs, values, and perceptions. Coach and author, Marie Forleo, calls this 'the master key.' She says:

 All you need is one core meta belief, a master key that unlocks every imaginable door in the castle of your consciousness. It's like throwing a switch that instantly illuminates a field of infinite potential.

I love this empowering metaphor. Forleo's core belief is that 'everything is figureoutable,' a philosophy she learnt from her very resilient mother. As she points out, this is a particularly useful mantra, not only conceptually, but practically too; I've used it recently to find a solution for everything from business woes to interior design conundrums. It's no surprise that the quote above comes from Forleo's book, which is called ... wait for it ... *Everything is Figureoutable.*

If I were to articulate my own master key, it would be something along these lines:

Everything is unfolding precisely as it should.

This mantra has become like a beacon for me, calling me home when I feel lost, anchoring me when I feel anxious. When I was a little girl, I loved saying my prayers. I particularly loved praying to the Virgin Mary, whom I adored. It was so comforting in times of upheaval or distress to feel as though I was *doing* something; I wasn't just sitting back and waiting to be swept along by events, passive and helpless. I had a direct line to whomever was calling the shots, and I could speak to them whenever I wanted.

My mantra has a similar effect for me these days. In contrast to the unquestioning faith of an innocent child, it's a consciously chosen belief. I have chosen to believe that life unfolds in a meaningful, purposeful way, even if we cannot understand or see that purpose from our vantage-point. I choose this belief because I think it's a beautiful way to view life, because my logical brain buys into it, and because to believe otherwise is not an option for me. If life is meaningless, directionless, and utterly random, then that's not a reality in which I can thrive or even survive. This mantra protects me, and it empowers me to accept the events in my life and run with them. Finally, it shapes my perceptions and therefore moulds my reality.

Do you have a master key? Do you have a world-view or philosophy that grounds you and makes sense of everything around you? I suspect that most of us do, whether or not we've articulated it, even to ourselves. Some of us will have inherited our world-view from our religion or from our parents or other figures of authority. Sometimes these are empowering models that arm us and give us the super-powers we need to get through life. Sometimes, however, they are out-of-date or limiting.

Unlike when I was a student, there isn't much opportunity to chat with friends about the meaning of life these days; we're often too bogged down in the mud to see the big picture. I mentioned in the Introduction, that butterflies have an enviable view-point. They can see into the distance and explore the bigger picture. Now that we have metamorphosed, we have the tools we need to choose a loftier vantage-point.

Take some time to think about your most fundamental views on life. Do you have a strong view about why we are here as a race, and why you are here as a person? Are these beliefs inherited or have you arrived at them over the years? My own inherited views have made way for beliefs that feel inherently right in my bones. What's more, they are not fixed. I'm still working so many things out. They ebb and flow. I refine them and reformulate them as I read more and as I grow as a person.

I'm not afraid to change my beliefs and I'm not afraid to cherry-pick from wise teachers and from diverse organised religions. I embrace the Catholic belief in guardian angels, while many Buddhist and Zen teachings have been invaluable in helping me to reduce my attachments to things, people, and outcomes. I am opportunistic in taking on board whatever helps me to navigate my way though life, and I urge you to do the same. Have fun with the learning process, broaden your inputs and your perspectives, and write your own blueprint for this crazy, amazing world as you grow.

Moving from Perception to Objectivity

Our perceptions limit our perspectives. Our unconscious biases limit our objectivity. Who knows if it's even possible to be objective?

On a business course, I had my eyes opened to the power of our unconscious biases, particularly something called 'anchoring' bias. We were put into small teams of five or six on each table and asked to work together to estimate various data-points. One was the average height of the redwood tree. We had three options. We could accept one of the two suggested answers: 180 feet or 200 feet, or we could offer our own suggestion.

As we went around the room calling out our answers, a curious phenomenon emerged. The estimates of the redwood tree's height ricocheted between two very different figures: around 190 feet and around 900 feet. What on earth was going on? It turned out that all of the teams on my side of the room had received the 'suggestions' that 180 or 200 feet were the plausible answers. The 'suggestions' that the teams on the other side of the room received were, on the other hand, either 800 or 1,000 feet. Unconsciously, we had all played safe and stuck closely to the anchors we'd been given when making our assessments. None of us wanted to put our heads above the parapet.

We use anchoring biases all the time, not only when estimating, but when creating perceptions. Relativity is such a critical part of how we view ourselves in the world. In Tim Ferriss' book, *Tools of Titans*, Naval Ravikant offers the following advice:

 If you want to be successful, surround yourself with people who are more successful than you are. If you want to be happy, surround yourself with people who are less successful.

I noticed that this applied to my kids too. For his first two years at school, my son Paddy attended a very prestigious pre-prep school. The mothers on the school run dripped with Gucci, Chloe, and even Chanel Couture. After a playdate at a friend's particularly jaw-dropping home, Paddy asked me, 'Mummy, why don't we have an elevator in our house?' Ok then. Time to move schools!

In a school jammed full of the sons of oligarchs and celebrities, we were one of the (very) least wealthy families there. We had many reasons for switching Paddy to the lovely little state school around the corner from us, but a big driver was building a healthy perception for him and our daughter Tilly, who attends the same school. We, and they, are blessed and privileged. We wanted them to be surrounded by a diverse mix of children and to understand their blessings. It's important to us that they appreciate what they have, while recognising that there will always be others with more than us. For their benchmark to be so fundamentally out of whack with the realities of the world was not acceptable.

It's hard to be objective when your benchmark is skewed. It's hard for our kids to understand how fortunate they are when they've had little exposure to real poverty. Our 'normal' is not other people's normal and yet it's the yardstick from which we form most of our perceptions.

This is why we can't trust our perceptions. We're far too close to the action to be objective. However, our perceptions determine our reality. Next, we're going to examine some ways in which we can change our reality today without changing a thing in our external world:

UPGRADING OUR LENSES

If our reality is, in fact, manufactured then we may as well manufacture ourselves a good one. If we can choose the lens through which we view our world, then let's pick a lens that depicts our world in glorious technicolour.

There are three lenses powerful enough to transform what we see before us:

1. Gratitude and appreciation
2. Joy, light, and optimism
3. Love and compassion

The next chapter covers Love in detail. For now, let's examine the first two lenses and understand how we can use them to change our focus. Think of these tools as acting like physical lenses. Our perceptions limit our vision; we only see part of the picture. These lenses throw the truly important aspects of life into sharp relief. What once was blurry becomes distinct.

1. GRATITUDE: THE MOST POWERFUL REFRAMING TOOL YOU'LL EVER NEED

One New Year's Eve, I was scrolling through Instagram and saw a post featuring the phrase, 'The things you take for granted, other people are praying for.' These words will stay with me forever. If I ever need a reality check on just how full of blessings my life is, this phrase acts like a proverbial kick up the backside. What do I take for granted *every single day*? Liberty. Sanitation. Freedom of speech. A roof over my head. A loving husband. Healthy children. My own health. My fridge full of food. A benign climate in the UK, free from extreme weather events.

I could go on, but you get the idea. These things form part of my reality and are as normal to me as the air that I breathe. I don't give thanks for them as often as I should. There but for the grace of God, I could be living in a dictatorship, suffering the effects of famine, in chronic pain, or trying to keep my children alive in a refugee camp. This is not to say that we should torture ourselves with 'what if's,' but it should remind us all that even our baseline reality contains multitudes of blessings.

Practicing gratitude is the easiest and most effective way to upgrade your perspective. Existing in a state of resignation to your surroundings will dull your senses. Existing in a state of gratitude, and holding dear even the most familiar parts of your daily reality, will open those senses to the wonders and blessings around you. Einstein's many words of wisdom particularly spoke to me when writing this chapter. As well as the quote that forms the epigraph to this chapter, another of his insights also resonated with me:

 There are only two ways to live your life. One is as though nothing is a miracle. The other is as though everything is a miracle.

On this basis, the world around you remains entirely

unchanged, but within you lie two utterly distinct ways of perceiving that world.

Making Your Reticular Activating System Work for You

Have you ever noticed that when you decide to get a new car, you suddenly see your chosen model everywhere you go? Or you get pregnant, and it seems as though there are bumps and pushchairs all around? This is down to our RAS, or Reticular Activating System. It's our brain's way of filtering through all the inputs it receives to show us what it thinks will be most relevant and useful. We may have seen hundreds of that new Mercedes model on the streets, but until it comes onto our radar, our brain may not have bothered to point it out for us.

Our RAS loves to work with gratitude. As we start to work on upgrading our perceptions, polishing up those dull senses, and bringing awareness and gratitude to certain parts of our lives, our RAS will excitedly bring more of these instances to our attention, like an eager puppy laying gifts at our feet. If we start to look up more and notice the amazing rooftop architecture in London, we'll find more and more examples that make our hearts sing. If we quieten down and take the time to drink up our child's belly-laugh, that gorgeous sound will start to cut through every other sensory input competing for our attention. If we pay more attention to our spouse's small, quiet acts of kindness, we will notice and love each act more.

Your RAS is equally adept at serving up your disappointments, failures, and resentments. What you project on your inner screen is entirely within your control.

I Don't Have To; I Get To

Neuro-linguistic programming, or NLP, has, at its core, the belief that 'the map is not the territory.' If the territory is reality, then our own perception of reality is the map and is by definition distorted, limited, and unique. We can use NLP techniques to manipulate that map by reframing a given situation.

I'm going to show you an effective way to upgrade your perceptions around anything for which you feel less than grateful. I find that this technique chimes well with the concept of other people praying for the things I take for granted. It's this: Don't say 'I have to.' Say 'I get to.' Here are a couple of examples of ways in which I reprogramme my attitude when I'm resisting something:

'I *have to* cook dinner for my kids':

My kids are very fussy eaters, and feeding them is a total and utter ball-ache.

'I *get to* cook dinner for my kids.':

First, I *get to* have two beautiful, healthy children. I am so fortunate. I know how many people have not been blessed with the children they want so badly. Second, I *get to* walk into a beautiful supermarket, laden with incredible fresh produce, flash my plastic, and buy *whatever I want.* Again, that's a luxury that only a tiny proportion of the world's population can even imagine. Third, I have an amazing husband who works long hours so that I *get to* work flexibly on wonderful projects like this book while having the time and opportunity to cook for my family. Believe me, I have to tell myself this pretty much every teatime, but it does reduce my resistance and increase my appreciation!

Get how this works? Let's try another example.

'I *have to* take loads of supplements':

As I mentioned, Chris and I are on a tonne of supplements as part of our functional health journey. I take up to thirty pills a day. I hate taking them; they make me gag and it's a pain in the ass.

'I get to take loads of supplements':

I *get to* see an amazing functional doctor and benefit from her expertise. I *get to* buy my supplements from the best sources, as recommended by her. I *get to* put into my body the *exact* substances that it needs to treat my deficiencies. I *get to* use these incredible tools to restore my optimal health and energy. I *get to* rebuild my gut lining/ treat my thyroid/ restore my hormone levels. I *get to* demonstrate my total commitment to my health every day.

The above can be translated as: most of the time, we don't know we're born. We forget how many blessings we have because they are our normal. It's not until our boiler breaks that we miss our hot showers. It's often not until our body gets sick that we realise how much we take good health for granted. For the majority of people reading this book, life is full of blessings. By upgrading our perception to gratitude at every possible moment, we can see the familiar in a new way.

How to Upgrade to Gratitude:

Micro-mindfulness. Stop in the moment. Smell the roses. Look at the perfect curve of your baby's cheek or your partner's backside. Use your senses with abandon; *revel* in the sensory pleasure of the food you're chopping or the book you're reading. Bury your nose into your sleeping child and drink up their scent. Flood yourself with gratitude for this sensory experience. Feel the *wonder* of the moment: this is living.

. . .

Keep it Clean. Use gratitude to fill you up and drive out lesser emotions. To the extent that you can, keep it a clean emotion. Essentially, you're upgrading your emotional state this way. I use gratitude to drive out, in particular, irritation and anxiety. If one of my kids is pushing my buttons, I find I can keep my shit together much more effectively if I tune out what's annoying me and just wallow in, and give thanks for, how gorgeous they are.

I also actively try to use gratitude to drown out anxiety. I find it very easy for love and anxiety to co-exist as a parent. I look at my children sleeping and I'm filled with a rush of love, which can be followed almost immediately by the cold dread of 'what if?' What if they get sick? What if they die? My happiness is so dependent on their wellbeing that it terrifies me. By consciously focusing on feeling waves of gratitude for their existence in this present moment, I find that I can upgrade my state from (unfounded) anxiety to a warm sense of peace and wellbeing.

Journal on Gratitude. Gratitude journals have been having a moment for some time now, and with good reason. Noting down what you're grateful for on a regular basis is extremely rewarding and beneficial. I like to take it further and wax lyrical about whatever it is I'm practicing gratitude for, rather than just noting it. Chip Franks, who works on *The Miracle Morning* with Hal Elrod, suggests journaling around appreciation of any of the following: something profound, something you take for granted, a current challenge or obstacle, people in your life, and past or upcoming events. In this way, we get to experience events, loved ones, and precious moments over and over again.

Meditate on Gratitude. Gratitude meditations are known to increase heart-rate variability (HRV) which is a measure of your heart's coherence and resilience. You can practice this easily at home with a tracker. I find that many trackers are more suited to exercising and I use the HeartMath tracker which is designed for meditating. It clips onto my ear lobe and syncs with my phone, giving me real-time feedback on whether I'm in a state of coherence or not. Even my kids can do it!

Imagine the warm, swelling feeling that you get in your heart when you think of someone you love or you do a good deed. That warm glow is your heart's coherence in action. Meditating on gratitude has so many health benefits, and is one of the easiest ways to meditate effectively.

Don't Count Sheep; Count Your Blessings. If you're having problems nodding off or your brain won't quieten down, counting or listing your blessings in detail across all areas of your life is a wonderful way to activate your para-sympathetic ('rest and digest') nervous system and it also primes your subconscious for happiness and wellbeing before heading into dreamland.

2. JOY, LIGHT AND OPTIMISM

There may be some of us who are naturally like Pollyanna, born optimists. I'm not one of those people and I'm pretty sure my daughter Tilly got the same memo. Her 'what if' questions are highly creative; that little girl can dream up a worst-case scenario out of absolutely nowhere.

No, for me it is a conscious choice every day to face life with joy and optimism. Einstein, who appears to be the star of this chapter, said the following:

 The most important decision we make is whether we believe we live in a friendly or hostile universe.

I revisit this quote almost daily. I agree that this decision is absolutely critical in establishing how we perceive our reality. I also agree that it is indeed a decision, whether or not we make it consciously.

How do you feel when you read this quote? Have you thought before about the fact that this decision is yours to make? Have you made this decision for yourself, and which side of the line did you fall on? Do you believe that the world is a cruel place where meaningless horrors befall good people or do you take the view, like Gabby Bernstein, that 'the universe has your back'?

Positivity is a *Choice*.

While we cannot control much of what happens in our life, we can choose the lens through which we look at life and this makes all the difference in the world.

I have made a conscious choice to wake up every day and view my life from a place of optimism and joy. I have only gravitated to this decision over the last few years; before that, I didn't even realise it was a decision I could make. I hadn't been told that 'to worry is to pray for what you do not want.' I'd never heard the serenity prayer used by twelve-step programmes. I was a natural worrier and I worried about *everything*, within and beyond my control.

The choice I've made is a really tough one. It's tough because it goes against all my natural instincts. I have to swallow my terror constantly. I have to battle my demons every day. However, I have found that with each day, it gets easier and easier. This is because I'm making it habitual to be positive. I'm rewiring my neural networks and it's working. I'm overwriting my instincts with my healthier emotional reactions and I'm finding it gradually more effortless to keep the wolves from the door.

Who are the wolves? For me they are anxiety and intrusive thoughts. I have suffered from both for decades, though they were at their most debilitating when I was between ten and thirteen years old. My guess is that the chemical upheaval of puberty was in many ways to blame, as the darkest time I've had since then was after the birth of my first child; postpartum being another classic period of hormonal hell. While biochemistry was in all likelihood the biggest driver of my suffering, the lack of understanding or coping mechanisms that I had at my disposal were huge compounding factors for me.

I want to tell you a little about my intrusive thoughts because they help explain my unwavering commitment to optimism, joy, and my mental, emotional, and spiritual health. I define intrusive thoughts as those thoughts that won't leave you alone despite the fact that *they are precisely the opposite of what you want to think.*

When I was a pre-teen, I would torture myself with 'what ifs.' What if Mum has a car-crash on the way home from work and doesn't make it back? What if I say something horrible to this person whom I love, to upset them? What if I throw myself out of the window? These thoughts never really went away, but after I gave birth to Paddy, they returned with a vengeance. What if he died of cot death? What if I accidentally left him on a bus? What if I left him on a bus on purpose? What if I'd accidentally put the covers too close to his little face and he suffocated in the night?

To be very clear, I didn't want to do any of these things. I didn't want any of them to happen. But the power that we have to wreck our own lives and those around us is absolutely terrifying, and the power that the universe has to destroy our lives and those of our loved ones is equally unthinkable. When you don't have the right coping mechanisms in place, this contradictory and sickening combination of utter helplessness and unwanted power is something that I know many of us struggle to handle. The tragedy has been that for so much of my life I've felt completely in the throes of these mysterious and unwelcome intruders.

A few years ago, I was reading a magazine and there was an article on a phenomenon called 'intrusive thoughts.' As I read it, I broke down in tears. Here were the demons that had haunted me for decades, named and shamed in black and white. Intrusive thoughts are a form of Obsessive Compulsive Disorder. This made sense to me as I have certainly manifested other signs of OCD in life. These include compulsive physical ticks as well as checking whether I'd left the cooker on, for example. I suspect I am not alone here.

The article detailed examples of people far more tormented by intrusive thoughts than I was. One woman had stopped riding in the car with her partner because she was so afraid of her unwanted compulsion to reach over and turn the steering wheel, pulling them into the next lane of traffic on the motorway. I couldn't believe that my demons had a name. I had found that the implications of the thoughts – namely the fear that I was mentally ill – had tortured me almost more than the thoughts themselves. But here was *Grazia* magazine calling them out, implying that they were common enough to warrant an article on them.

When I told my husband that night about my revelation, and defined intrusive thoughts for him, he replied: 'But everybody has those thoughts!' This was both a remarkable lightbulb moment for me and a huge blow. All this time, I'd been thinking I was damaged and alone, and, all this time, I was neither. I was normal. It seemed to me that I could cope with the thoughts themselves, if I didn't have to worry so much about their implications.

Since I read that article, society has made huge strides in opening up about mental health. Journalist Bryony Gordon has spoken at length about her heartbreaking struggles with OCD, especially in the wake of new motherhood, and has done incredible work to provide a platform to others suffering. Most notably, she launched her Mad World podcast with an interview with Prince Harry to discuss the devastating mental impact that losing his mother has had on him.

The real strides I have made have not come from dealing directly with my intrusive thoughts and anxiety. They've been as a result of my reading and the work I've done on myself over the last three years. By recalibrating my view of the world, by learning more about a type of spirituality that speaks to me, by building up an arsenal of incredible tools such as meditation, journaling, prayer, affirmations, mindfulness, self-love, and self-compassion, I've created a perspective on life that serves me and supports me.

Now you can see why Einstein's quote means so much to me. For almost three decades I felt like a victim of circumstance, and of the vagaries of my mind. I felt utterly at the whim of whatever the universe wanted to throw at me.

Today I choose to believe that the universe is a friendly place, a kind place, and an environment in which I can thrive without looking over my shoulder constantly.

I believe this both spiritually and intellectually. The beauty of the modern age is that so much scientific and spiritual theory can be reconciled through quantum physics. What we now know about energy sits easily with a belief in miracles, in synchronicity, and in the inter-connectedness of us all. We don't have to choose between science and spirituality, as so many thinkers before us had to do. I include some suggestions of further reading that is informative but not offputtingly technical, online at www.healthy-wealthyandwiseuk.com/met.

The way Einstein puts it, believing in a friendly universe is no bigger leap of faith than believing in a hostile universe. But the rewards of taking the former stance are incredible. These days, I am in possession of a framework that comforts and supports me, and allows me to go through my days without being held captive by anxiety.

I realise that many of us cling to worry as a defence mechanism: if I expect the worst, then it will hurt less if it does happen. However, the worst case will hurt regardless, and meanwhile we've wasted huge swathes of time imprisoned in fearful fantasies for no good reason. In the UK, it's a cliché that builders and scaffolders on a building site will yell out: 'Cheer up love! It may never 'appen!' to any less-than-cheerful-looking passers-by. I think the builders may be onto something.

Last night we were driving back to London from my in-laws' in Kent. We'd had a late family lunch and, as it's December at the time of writing this chapter, the night was drawing in very early. I'd given Chris the go-ahead to have a couple of drinks with his lunch on the basis that I would drive. I hate driving in the dark, especially on motorways. I find it disorientating and far harder than in good light. All afternoon, I could feel the anxiety rising up in me. I was tense before and during lunch, willing it to come to a close so we could get on the road.

Five years ago, I would have spiralled further; my imagination would have run riot and imagined us all dying in a horrible car-crash as I misjudged a lane-change in the dark. Yesterday, I called on my resources. I breathed, I named the fear, and I focused on Einstein's words. Statistically, the chances of us crashing were tiny. I am a careful and competent driver and I knew intellectually that I could get us home safely. I chose to seek refuge in the fact that this is a good universe which has my back, and that our 'teams of light' (which is the beautiful phrase that psychic medium Laura Lynne Jackson has for our deceased loved ones and guardian angels) were there to protect us. I stayed very present on the drive home and I even managed to relax enough to marvel at the spectacular sunset as we drove west (perhaps it was my team of light putting on a show of reassurance for me). And, do you know, I got us home safely.

This, really, is how our perceptions can shape our reality. Our attitude to life, or our mindset, dictates so much of how our days pan out. Gabby Bernstein says in *Super Attractor*:

 I've come to believe that the only way out of that world of darkness is to choose to see the light as often as possible. Seeing the light is a practice, and it requires our willingness to suspend our disbelief.

The daily choice to believe in optimism, light, and joy, and to bathe myself in gratitude, pays me enormous dividends. The greatest of these dividends is my ability to enjoy my life and count my blessings. Without these tools, it's entirely likely that I would be too busy worrying about the future to remember to wonder at the present. Our life is already amazing. We just have to notice it.

You can check out my favourite books and other resources for Perception is Reality at www.healthywealthyandwiseuk.com/met

8

LOVE: REFRAMING HOW WE SEE OTHERS

If there is any meaning in life greater than connecting with other human beings, I haven't found it.

Melinda Gates

Melinda Gates' quote from *The Moment of Lift* is a world apart from the infamous words with which Jean-Paul Sartre ended his play *The Exit:* 'Hell is other people!' These two attitudes illustrate the inherent conflict facing the human race. We are mammals who require human connection just to survive, and yet our interactions with others can cause pain as easily as they bring joy.

In the last chapter, we examined how upgrading our perceptions to a vantage point of gratitude and appreciation, joy and optimism, can reframe our entire experience of life without actually changing any of our physical reality. I believe that upgrading our perceptions of others is equally critical to deriving the maximum pleasure and value from life.

The purpose of this chapter is to establish tools that empower us to turn our relationships with others into a source of joy and strength. At this stage in our journey we've metamorphosed to the extent that we have far more self-awareness than we did. We've chosen consciousness, we've recognised the importance of taking full responsibility, and we've learnt how to exercise self-discipline. All of these learnings will prove invaluable in our relationships.

Remember, we're still perched on the branch that once held our cocoon. We're poised for flight but we are taking stock before we spread our wings; we're revelling in the fact that we have a much broader perspective after our metamorphosis and we're using what we've learnt to recalibrate our perception of our world. We're seeing with new eyes, and, as we gaze around us, what once was tired and familiar may start to feel fresh.

This chapter moves from observing the macro, which is the case for human interconnectedness, to the micro, or the everyday, close-up interactions that we have with our fellow human beings. We've seen how, by changing the way that we look at things, those things can change. Now it's time to look at human connection with a new, elevated lens: the lens of love.

THE CASE FOR HUMAN CONNECTION

We Need Human Connection to Survive and Thrive

Human connection is a biological imperative, and science shows us that we can affect each other far more than we may realise. So many of our vital functions, from healing to creativity, require us to feel safe and connected. This is a function of our vagus nerve, which controls our autonomic nervous system. When stimulated, the vagus nerve activates our parasympathetic nervous system ('rest and digest'). The better our vagal tone, the more easily we can switch on our parasympathetic nervous system after a stressor.

When we mobilise our sympathetic nervous system, we're in fight-or-flight mode. This means our body prioritises the functions needed to fight or flee at the expense of other functions such as our immune and digestive systems. We can't heal, digest, or create when we're under stress.

I've read a few books on achieving creativity and productivity within teams. These include *The Culture Code* by Daniel Cole, *Dare to Lead* by Brené Brown. and *Creativity Inc.*, the story of Pixar by its founder Ed Catmull. A common thread struck me: in order to produce great, creative work, we need to feel safe. Once I read Stephen Porges' *Pocket Guide to Polyvagal Theory,* I understood why this is the case.

As I mentioned above, when we're in fight-or-flight mode we are operating with a tightly edited set of bodily functions. We are in emergency mode; we simply cannot thrive. Think of the parallel with managing your workload. Projects that are important but not urgent tend to get sidelined by urgent tasks. Our bodies operate in a similar way. When we feel stressed, we are not in homeostasis, and essential, but less urgent, functions are paused. We're in a defensive state that cannot coexist with a growth state.

But what does this have to do with human connectivity? As mammals, we rely heavily on each other for the necessary social cues to allow ourselves to feel safe. As Porges puts it, we 'reciprocally regulate each other's physiological state'. He explains: 'Basically, our nervous system craves reciprocal interaction to enable state regulation to feel safe.'

In other words, our nervous systems are designed to require certain social interaction with fellow humans to generate the necessary safety cues. And when we get them, we can thrive. This is because *the neural pathways of social behaviour and interaction are the same neural pathways that we use to support healing and growth.*

The positive effect of having social or familial support when recovering from illness or injury has been well documented. Porges says:

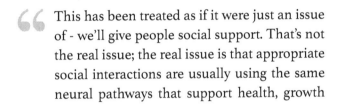

> This has been treated as if it were just an issue of - we'll give people social support. That's not the real issue; the real issue is that appropriate social interactions are usually using the same neural pathways that support health, growth and restoration.

In short, we can help to heal each other because the benefits of social interaction on our nervous system are so great. In the same way that chronic stress is known to play utter havoc on our bodies, human connection is a critical way for us to demobilise our sympathetic nervous system and access a state where we can heal and grow.

Malcolm Gladwell illustrated this point in *Outliers* when he investigated the citizens of Roseto, Pennsylvania. The community was entirely composed of emigrants from Roseto Valfortore in Italy. The town boasted an exceedingly low rate of disease despite a less than ideal diet, as well as obesity and smoking. Local scientists concluded that the exceptional level of social interaction and support among everyone in the community was the likely cause of its good health.

Our Energies Connect Us All

We know that we can connect and communicate with each other in ways that we cannot always explain. It's been suggested that women in close proximity tend to regulate their menstrual cycles to coincide, as do female dogs. Premature twins thrive more when they lie next to each other. The power of group prayer has been well-documented on various occasions. We think of a friend and they call us out of the blue. When someone tells us a story, our neurons can mirror those of the storyteller. Scientific tests show that our heart waves can affect someone else's brain waves, and vice versa.

In her book, *Energy Medicine*, Jill Blakeway details Princeton University's Engineering Anomalies Research (PEAR) programme, which created a random event generator machine (REG). Over 28 years of experiments, the programme showed that humans could affect the machine's numerical output in a tiny but statistically significant way. What's more, two people working with the machine had a stronger effect than one, and a couple that was emotionally attached had the strongest effect of all.

Since PEAR shut its doors, the Global Consciousness Project has undertaken many similar experiments, in particular around large-scale, emotional events such as New Year's Eve and Trump's inauguration. The GCP finds that while compassion is one of the most effective emotions as far as the REGs' data output is concerned, fear also drives data deviations. Blakeway quotes Roger Nelson, creator of the GCP, as saying that 'we are designed to be interconnected.

And there is a potential awakening for us, to reach a more unified field of consciousness, to create a layer of intelligence for the earth.'

Thanks to quantum physics, we know that we are not matter; we are composed of pure energy. We are forged from the stars. I don't believe it's a big leap to see that we are all interconnected. I'm not sure that many of us, myself included, spend enough time pondering on how deeply we can connect with each other beyond the physical realm, or why we co-exist in this interconnected way.

In my view, some of the most beautiful and meaningful explanations for both the cause and form of our human connections come from people who've experienced the other side of life: that is, death. Psychic medium Laura Lynne Jackson has greatly impacted my world-view with her beautiful books, *The Light Between Us* and *Signs.* Jackson's incredible gift has given her a perspective on life that the majority of us lack. In fact, she argues that we only see around fifteen percent of what is around us on earth: 'The rest is unseen energy and light connections.'

Jackson believes that 'earth is a school where we are all learning a collective lesson in love. We are spiritual beings here to learn about connectivity and kindness.' She elaborates that we are not just following our own paths; we intersect with others' paths, allowing us many opportunities to add meaning to each other's lives. She talks a good deal about the cords of love and light that bind us in, and beyond, this life. Her books don't just detail what happens to us and our loved ones when we cross; they paint a beautiful picture of why we're here, what actually matters in life, and why the connection between us all on earth is so much stronger than our logical, Newtonian frameworks can possibly illustrate.

If Jackson's impression of life is valid, then there is absolutely nothing that matters more than human connection. There is nothing more worthwhile or noble than leaning into our gloriously messy, flawed, and complex fellow human beings and in doing so, weaving 'a magical tapestry of meaning and love and forgiveness and hope and light with each other', to quote her once more.

Jackson's world-view is very similar to that of Anita Moorjani, who, as I mentioned in Chapter 6, returned from a near-death experience (NDE) to find her body rapidly shedding all signs of the cancer that had taken her to multiple organ-failure. Since her NDE, her world-view has completely and utterly transformed. She sees now that: 'in the tapestry of life, we're all connected. Each one of us is a gift to those around us, helping each other to be who we are, weaving a perfect picture together.' Her understanding now is that the universe is made up of unconditional love, and we are all part of that love which means we cannot be separate from each other. We are all one.

As you can see, I somewhat fell down a rabbit-hole of reading about the afterlife; I read Jackson's two books and *Dying to be Me* in quick succession. I have to say that reading them gave me a transformative perspective-shift. In the next chapter we'll talk about choosing models of reality that serve us. What if the world is a place full of miracles that we're choosing to ignore? As we discussed, Einstein reminded us that we can live our lives as though nothing, or everything, is a miracle. What if my sense of duality from other humans is a false perception, and I am tied to everyone I pass by cords of love and light? What if I could open myself up to see the light in everyone? In a world where we are fully at liberty to choose and use the models of reality that serve us best, I find this to be a magical perspective that elevates the meaning of my human inter-actions.

Wherever your beliefs fall, from a physical perspective we all share the same fabric; our bodies can welcome each other's blood and organs. Whatever perceptions of 'us and them' we manufacture, we're all made of the same stuff. We really are no different inside. However, human strife feels as inevitable as it does timeless. So what's going on?

ADDRESSING THE OBSTACLES TO HUMAN CONNECTION

As far as I can see, the ways in which we cause one another grief fall into six categories:

1. **Duality:** we feel separate from each other.

2. **Self-centredness:** often, it feels as though others are less 'real' than us.

3. **Communication:** or the lack of it.

4. **Judgement:** we struggle to accept others' differences from us, and we judge them.

5. **Hurt:** we let others hurt us and devalue us.

6. **Empathy:** when we over-empathise, we feel too much pain on others' behalf.

Let's take these in turn, defining each area of conflict and examining solutions that will strengthen the bonds of our human connections. In many cases, you'll find that the skills you've acquired in Part I will be foundational to these solutions.

1. Duality

It seems to me that almost every problem we encounter with our fellow humans comes down to duality: the idea that we are separate from each other. Above, I made the case for why the worlds of science and spirituality don't see it this way. But however compelling these lofty ideals are, we often feel conflicted when we move from the macro to the micro, from intellectually espousing ideals to implementing them in our everyday.

No matter how deeply we understand that we are all the same inside, often it's our differences that seem the most marked on the surface. If people look or speak differently from us, have different habits and customs, and approach life in a way that feels alien, it can be hard to establish common ground. If universal consciousness is the ocean, and we are all drops in that ocean, then it follows that we are all inextricably connected in one-ness. However, duality is a construct of our ego, which fights desperately against this one-ness. Our ego wants us to believe that we are separate from everything, and therefore from everyone: it persists with the illusion of separation.

Psychologist, teacher, and author, Tara Brach, argues that the perception of difference is part of our evolutionary survival toolbox, that we read behaviours, looks, and mannerisms as ways to establish whether someone is part of our tribe. In her book, *Radical Acceptance,* she says: 'While this evolutionary conditioning to perceive difference is powerful, we also have the capacity to relax our armor. We can enlarge our sense of tribe.'

Brené Brown, who has made compassion and whole-heartedness a cornerstone of her life's work, puts it brilliantly: 'People are hard to hate close-up. Move in.' One-ness is much easier to think about than to practice. This is a major shift to make. While we may believe philosophically that one-ness is a superior ideology to duality, it's hard to actually practice one-ness in daily life, when people are pissing us off left, right, and centre. As Brown says, the only way to turn one-ness from a thought into a deed is to move in and get close to our fellow humans. The next five areas are all manifestations of how our dualistic approach plays out, so let's take them in turn and explore how to upgrade both our perceptions of, and relationships with, each other.

2. Self-centredness

In Chapter 1, we discussed the fact that our unconsciousness puts us firmly at the centre of our own narrative. When our ego runs the show, it reinforces our perception that others are not only separate from us, but are supporting actors, bit-players in our own drama. We and our problems are cast in sharp relief; others are less distinct. I find that when we are struggling with our own problems, be they ill-health or stresses, our self-absorption becomes even more pronounced; our issues take centre-stage and as we obsess over them we leave ourselves less and less bandwidth to accommodate the needs of others in our lives, even close family and friends.

Brach articulates this phenomenon perfectly in *Radical Acceptance* (as an aside, I cannot recommend this breath-taking book more highly). She calls it 'the trance of the unreal "other."' Brach observes, 'When we are caught in our own self-centred drama, everyone else becomes "other" to us, different and unreal.' This encapsulates perfectly the price that others pay when we become enslaved to our own relentless internal narratives.

I also think Brach's definition of others as unreal helps to illuminate how we can hurt others more easily. Throughout history, it has served us to see entire cultures and races as 'unreal,' so different from us as to be less than human and therefore easier to harm. In the age-old phenomenon of 'us and them,' 'them' invokes a faceless tribe that is fair game because they're unreal. It's not so easy to hurt people up-close.

I've always loved the story of the Christmas Day Truce during World War I. The tale has captured the hearts of many and has been analysed at length. It's essentially an account of how people temporarily stopped being unreal in each other's eyes and, for a precious few hours, became real-life, flesh-and-blood humans with hopes, fears, and loved-ones back home. We're all far more similar than we are different; our pleasures and pains are universal.

Sonder, Not Solipsism

It's hard for our brains to process that billions of people on the planet can all, simultaneously, lead a life that is as rich and varied as our own. It's almost easier to believe in meta-physical solipsism, which is the philosophy that the self is the only reality, and that our world and other people only exist as representations of ourselves, and have no independent existence.

I was much younger when I came across this concept and I remember being terrified by it; it felt like the most isolating idea in the world. Now I find it obnoxiously ego-centric. It is truly the antithesis of the idea that we are all connected and interwoven in one consciousness. I choose connection.

If solipsism paints all others as unreal, then sonder is a concept that makes our fellow humans shine as three-dimensional beings. The word *sonder* was only coined in 2012 by John Koenig; it's new enough that my computer keeps auto-correcting it to *wonder*. A Google search throws up the following definition: sonder is 'The profound feeling of realizing that everyone, including strangers passed in the street, has a life as complex as one's own, which they are constantly living despite one's personal lack of awareness of it.'

Essentially, sonder is the understanding that all other humans lead an inner life whose richness and complexity is equal to ours. Unless we're into solipsism, we already know this intellectually, but it really does boggle the mind: billions of humans with unique and equally elaborate inner worlds. When we embrace this, we bring our fellow humans out of the shadows and into the limelight in our lives; we marvel at their unique qualities and we appreciate the ways in which, together, we can be so much greater than the sum of our parts.

Really Seeing People

We may often be guilty of not seeing the people who most easily blend into the background of our lives: waiters and waitresses, hotel maids, doormen, street-sweepers, delivery people, the homeless. If we are capable of relegating loved-ones to supporting roles in our lives, then these folks are in danger of being given the walk-on parts.

I've heard many times about Bill Clinton's incredible charisma, including from people who've met him in person. He is often described as making others feel like they're the only person in the room. He's the first person featured in Richard Reed's book, *If I Could Tell You Just One Thing,* and Reed reports being absolutely staggered by Clinton's unrelenting energy and commitment to the people they met on a gruelling charity trip to Africa. The one piece of advice that Clinton offers is:

I've come to believe that one of the most important things is to see people. The person who opens the door for you, the person who pours your coffee. Acknowledge them. Show them respect. The traditional greeting of the Zulu people of South Africa is 'Sawubona'. It means 'I see you'. I try and do that.

My takeaways from this are that, firstly, it's something Clinton does consciously and purposefully. He has made a commitment to deepening his human relationships by taking the time to recognise and connect with everyone that he meets, especially the most disenfranchised people on the planet. Secondly, like Melinda Gates, he finds the richest personal rewards in connecting with people who, to many, are invisible. Thirdly, these efforts are not only noticed but legendary. In a world where so many of us are playing out our own one-man drama, Clinton's choice to really see others is noteworthy.

Brach tells of one of her clients who, having struggled to lay aside her personal problems sufficiently to see others as real, discovered a wonderful tool. Whenever she passed or encountered someone, she would repeat to herself: 'You are real. You are real.' In this way she brought them to life for herself. When we bring other people to life, we do them a service but we also add vivid paint-strokes to our own world.

I believe that investing in deepening our human connections is one of the hardest and most rewarding commitments that we can undertake. When we examine how to identify and live our values in the next chapter, you'll see what I mean. Human connection is one of my two principal values, chosen for precisely the above reason: I know how important it is, and yet I have a tendency to resist it with every bone in my body.

When we shake ourselves awake from the ceaseless internal monologue that our ego delivers to us and consciously make an effort to weave ourselves more deeply into the tapestry of human inter-connection, the sparks really fly. Honestly, I've had some of my biggest chemical highs when I've taken the time to *see* a homeless person, squat down and ask them what they need. I've felt the warm glow when I've engaged with a lonely neighbour or struck up a brief but effusive chat with a waiter or sales-assistant in a store. Human connection lights up our brain's reward centre and raises our vibrational energy. It's the best drug out there.

3. Communication

My friend and coach, Charlotte, has the following words from George Bernard Shaw on her business cards: 'The single biggest problem in communication is the illusion that it has taken place.' This quote makes me want to both laugh and cry. It sums up so many of the obstacles to human connection.

We don't communicate sufficiently with each other for so many reasons. When we don't see others properly, we may not either pay sufficient attention to what *they* are trying to tell *us*, or deem it important enough to fully communicate *our* needs or views to *them*. As we covered in Chapter 6, we all have different, self-constructed rules by which we live our lives, and conflict often arises when we inadvertently break each other's rules. We regularly misconstrue each other's motives and agendas, often because we're so tied up in our own narratives. We do this even with people we love. We spend so much time inside our own heads that we have no hope of becoming equally familiar with the workings of other people's minds.

Brené Brown, whose books I think should be recommended reading for anyone over the age of sixteen and compulsory for anyone managing a team of people, has a couple of characteristically brilliant techniques for building open channels of communication. The first is clarity: 'Clear is kind. Unclear is unkind.' A hard 'no' is much kinder to the recipient than a 'maybe' that is really a 'no'.

It's no generalisation to say that we all fall short of communicating with optimum clarity. I've learnt it time and time again in business: I give someone a fuzzy brief and they take a stab at reading my mind, usually unsuccessfully. I've learnt it in parenting: if you've ever sent a kid upstairs to fetch something without being crystal-clear about what you want them to fetch, they'll either come downstairs empty-handed or get distracted by a toy and delayed indefinitely.

Brown's most brilliant technique though, is 'the story I'm telling myself'. Here are some examples:

'You guys all went along to the meeting without me and the story I'm telling myself is that I'm not a valued part of the team.'

You haven't told me you loved me for days and the story I'm telling myself is that you want a divorce.'

It's genius! It works for so many scenarios and so many different types of relationships. Its brilliance lies in the fact that it protects both parties. If I'm accusing a colleague of something, I want them to know I'm giving them the benefit of the doubt, and I don't want them to think I'm insane. 'The story I'm telling myself' is a wonderful way to build space to be vulnerable (Brown's speciality) and to be clear about your feelings while being open-hearted enough to understand that the other party may be entirely unaware of them.

There is a cartoon sketch I've seen. A man is lying along the flat top of a cliff-edge, trying to pull up by the arm a woman who is dangling off the side of the cliff. What the woman can't see is that there is an enormous boulder on top of the man, crushing him. Meanwhile, he is unaware of the fact that there's a serpent emerging from a niche in the cliff, threatening to poison the woman. Both are trying their best despite these pressures, but both are wondering why the other can't just try harder. By taking each other at face value we invariably miss a large part of each other's personal situation at any given time. We can't tell what each other is thinking, struggling with, suffering from, or assuming *unless* we start talking to each other.

Much of the time, the narratives we tell ourselves drown out what other people may be trying to communicate to us. Therefore, most of the work on improving this dynamic falls outside of this chapter. The good news is that, having come this far, we have so many tools at our disposal to improve our communication abilities and our relationships:

We become more conscious.

We wake up to and get curious about our internal narratives.

We're less quick to jump to conclusions about others' motives.

We have greater empathy for each other which allows us to see and hear each other more clearly.

We start to take responsibility for our actions and reactions; we no longer lash out and blame others for our misfortunes.

We begin to flex our self-discipline muscle more instinctively; we see the bigger picture in our relationships and choose to value that over the instant gratification of communicating negatively.

We cease to make every situation all about ourselves. As we shed our limiting beliefs, we cease to use others' words to reinforce those beliefs in our head. In this way, we hear more clearly what they actually have to say, rather than what we infer.

We can distil effective communication down to our ability to articulate our thoughts, opinions, and needs, and to listen effectively when others do the same. You'll find that as you've metamorphosed, your approach to communication has transformed too.

4. Judgement

I once read that we judge others the most in areas where we ourselves feel least secure. This makes sense, and it explains why we are so quick to judge each other's parenting styles in particular. Is there anything that breeds insecurity more effectively than our efforts to keep our children alive and raise them to be fully-functioning members of society? Thought not.

Therefore, parenting is an area rife with judgement. It's all relative, you see. If I am feeling inadequate as a parent and I spot someone giving their kid a chocolate bar on the way to school one morning, it's instant feedback for me. Well at least I'm not *that* bad. I'm not *that* kind of parent. We rate others using simplistic methods and we judge them for their perceived relative shortcomings. It's a see-saw; I can slam them down and instantly boost myself.

I want to tell you two things which are unfortunately not mutually exclusive. First, I think judgement is a toxic phenomenon that really underscores our duality, our sense of 'us and them.' It drives an artificial wedge between us based on constructs that are just not important. Second, despite my believing that, I'm aware that I tend to be extremely judgemental of others (and myself) in a myriad of ways, and I'm quick to judge, at that.

If I'm to agree with my opening paragraph in this section, then my tendency to judge must be at least partially due to my own insecurities. Certainly, women are each other's harshest judges and it's common for us to judge each other on every criterion from looks to breastfeeding choices to the career decisions we make after we have kids. I'm pretty sure that when I rush to judge someone else, it's a band-aid for a wound of deep insecurity and the inherent belief that I am not enough just as I am. The band-aid is a temporary fix. There's only one party harmed when we judge: ourselves. The recipient of our judgement is, usually, unaware of our indictments against them. The judgement leaves a bitter taste and a hollow feeling.

Of course, it is our ego doing the judging. The higher self, who knows that we are all part of a great, interwoven tapestry of light, is nowhere to be found at these moments. Our ego, whose job it is to ensure our individual needs are met, is intent on reinforcing ideas of duality and separation. And because it's a creature of chronic insecurity, it won't spare others pain to boost itself. The ego thinks in a binary way: us and them, right and wrong. We judge people who make different choices from us because our ego prefers to see them as wrong rather than ourselves.

In my case, I've found my judgemental behaviour to be, most often, an extension of my intrusive thoughts. Just as people with intrusive thoughts don't want any of the things they think about to actually happen, I don't want to think badly of others. Doing so makes me feel sick. But my habitual behaviour has been to let the negative thoughts slip in immediately, before I have time to consciously process a person or a situation. It's become second nature to sink into darkness and assume the worst – about others, and about any given situation.

The good news is that we know we can rewire habitual practices by committing to upgrading them to new practices that serve us better. There's only one way to drive out darkness: turn on the lights. In the case of judgement, the light comes in the form of love. When we reject ideas of duality and focus on love, there's no space for judgement.

There's a great trick that I was taught to drown out judgement and 'otherness.' When you see anyone – from a colleague to a cashier to someone on the street, say to yourself: 'I love him,' or 'I love her.' This instant light brings such a feeling of tenderness that it's pretty much impossible for judgemental feelings to sneak in. Sometimes I sit on the tube and do this. I love him. I love her. When I consciously realise that I'm starting to judge, I instantly start to bless everyone around me with love. When you feel loving towards your fellow humans it's easier to believe that everyone is, in fact, doing the best they can with whatever limited resources, perspective, and coping mechanisms they have. This, in turn, breeds compassion for them.

Compassion and judgement can't sit together. Love and compassion are a balm to the sting that is judging others. When we choose love, compassion, and the belief that everyone is doing the best they can, then we see our relationships and the broader human race with fresh eyes and an open heart.

152 | SARA MADDERSON

5. Hurt

We are all told that other people can't hurt us without our permission, but my God, it feels very hard to withdraw that permission. We know, for example, that we need to hear ten pieces of positive feedback to balance out every one piece of negative feedback that we receive. I only remember one thing about my first performance review at work in 2001. Of course, it was the single piece of 'constructive' feedback that lingered in my memory. I have no idea what else was said. If you're interested, the feedback was that I have no filter and should try to think more before I speak. I'm still working on that one!

One of the most helpful things to remember is that we can't control other people. We can't control what they do or think, and we can't control what they think *of us*. In *The Power of Intention,* Dr Dyer spells out why it's just plain impractical to care about other people's opinions. He explains that if he delivers a speech to five hundred people, then there will be five hundred opinions of him in the room. None of us can control that. The key is to focus on our own character and to ensure that we're acting with integrity. If we are, it's all good. If our critics have a valid point then we take 100% responsibility: we accept the criticism and own the process of making good on our faults.

At this stage in our journey we now have enough empathy for and connection with others to understand that we all have our own issues. If people in our lives lash out at us in anger, it's entirely likely that their anger is a symptom of their own personal struggles rather than anything we have done. I love the phrase 'hurt people hurt people.' Attack is the best form of defence.

We know we can't control the opinions of others, so we

surrender to them, because we also know that resistance is a great cause of pain in our lives. And, we know that when people hurt us, it often means they're in pain themselves. Finally, we know that when we have enough love and compassion for ourselves we don't let the opinions of others, good or bad, rattle us. When we know that we are enough just as we are, then we're freed from the tyranny of having to earn other people's good opinions. In *Letting Go: The Pathway to Surrender*, David Hawkins writes:

 ...the truly humble cannot be humbled. They are immune to humiliation. They have nothing to defend. There is no vulnerability and, therefore, the truly humble do not experience critical attacks by others. Instead, a truly humble person sees the critical verbalization by another person as merely a statement of the other person's inner problems.

We've covered the concept of self-worth in Chapter 6. I urge you to go back and revisit the section entitled: 'It Feels Like Unshakeable Self-Belief," which is the key to demobilizing the power of others to hurt you.

6. Empathy

The final way in which our human connections can cause hurt and anguish lies in our ability to overly empathise or identify with each other's suffering. Don't get me wrong; empathy is a cornerstone of conscious living. But when we're too wrapped up in other people's pain, we can't serve ourselves or society well. This is why we need to set ourselves boundaries.

I've always thought I would like to write a novel but have had very few decent ideas. The best concept I've come up with is a novel called *Empathy*, in which the heroine is so overly empathetic with others that she temporarily inhabits their bodies and essentially experiences their personal reality for a time. Of course, I imagine her journey through the eyes of others to yield life-changing perspectives to her. Maybe I'll write it someday.

My reason for mentioning this is that we all have moments where we walk past a homeless man or woman on a wet day, or watch mothers in Syrian refugee camps trying to keep their babies warm on TV. We think, 'there but for the grace of God go I,' but in real life we don't, thank God, inhabit the bodies of others. Instead, we search for a mechanism to limit our empathy; we have to forge ahead with our own lives despite the weight of others' suffering. But how is it possible for us to hold true compassion for others without buckling under their pain? And how can we enjoy our own good fortune without crippling guilt?

In *The Code of the Extraordinary Mind*, Vishen Lakhiani recalls the time that he and his wife met the Dalai Lama. His wife asked His Holiness pretty much the same questions as I've posed above. His answer: 'But who can you help if you're unhappy?'

It's true. If we're on earth to spread light and connect to others, we need compassion, but we also need to feel *good* in order to be of any value. In their book *We: A Manifesto for Women Everywhere*, Gillian Anderson and Jennifer Nadel remind us that:

True kindness comes from a spiritually aligned place. It involves standing in our own shoes and affording others the same dignity. If you find yourself obsessing about another's suffering, gently remind yourself to step back into your own life. You do not need to play God or feel their feelings. Do what you can and then let go of the results.

I like this advice because it benefits both parties. We shouldn't be trying to play God with another person's life. At the same time, we shouldn't be trying to control outcomes that are far beyond our control; that kind of resistance will just cause us pain. The Dalai Lama is, of course, right. When we feel good, when we are 'spiritually aligned' with the universe, when we are operating in the higher vibration energies of love and joy, we are much more useful to ourselves, our families, and others who need our care.

If this section is resonating with you, and you tend to over-empathise with others and suffer excessively through them, then I recommend Gabby Bernstein's book *Super Attractor*. The book extols the benefits of feeling good, and it's a lesson that I return to constantly. She says,

 We can't help or uplift anyone or anything else from a place of resistance and low vibration ... We're living in a time when we must bring more positivity and light to the world."

Choosing to feel good in the face of other people's sorrow, and bad things happening all around you, doesn't mean you're a sociopath or a narcissist. It means you're using your greatest powers for the greatest good.

IN CONCLUSION:

The human race is unlikely to become a beautiful tapestry of interconnectedness and light overnight. That said, the last six sections of this chapter have illustrated that so much of our conflict stems from seriously basic issues.

At the heart of all our problems is duality: we see everyone else as separate from us. This leads to us perceiving others as bit-parts in our own soap opera. Duality causes our failure to communicate fully and wholeheartedly with each other. It results in judgement of the ways in which others are different from us, and allows us to feel hurt or devalued based on other people's opinions.

Empathy comes from a different place and can be a sign of love and compassion but can often be a symptom of our own insecurity and lack of self-faith. When we're in a good place, we can choose to feel good about our blessings and use that positive energy to shine our light.

I believe that when we take the steps to elevate our own consciousness, the ripple-effects on our relationships, and on humanity, are beautiful and wide-spread. As Marianne Williamson says in her poem, *Our Deepest Fear*:

 And as we let our own light shine,
We unconsciously give other people permission to do the same.

You can check out my favourite books and other resources for Love: Reframing How We See Others at www.healthywealthyandwiseuk.com/met

9

WHAT DO WE ACTUALLY WANT FROM LIFE?

Happiness is the meaning and the purpose of life, the whole aim and end of human existence.

Aristotle

Why is the above question such a tough one to answer? It's because it's the million-dollar question, and the stakes are sky-high. We can so easily waste our life chasing the wrong things, or identifying what we think we need to be happy and refusing to be happy if that scenario doesn't materialise. Nothing is guaranteed to pile on the pressure like being asked to condense all of our hopes and dreams for life into a one-liner.

Here's the good news. While you may not find it easy to articulate exactly what you want in life just yet, you have likely started to see the world around you with new eyes as a result of your metamorphosis. While we worked through the steps of transformation in Part I, our perspective began to gradually shift. Then, the first two chapters of Part II presented an alternative way of discerning our current reality without making any physical changes. At this point in our journey, we are approaching life from an elevated position, more fully aware of our blessings, and we will experience gratitude, joy, wonder, love, and compassion where once we may have felt numb to what was around us.

It's so important to take pause to note these inner adjustments and to marvel at how much more wonderful life looks through these new lenses. Our glass may have gone from half-empty to half-full, or it may even be running over. When we're conscious enough to assess our life accurately, rather than from a blinkered place of victimhood, self-absorption, resentment, or scarcity, then we're in a much stronger position to make positive life choices moving forward. Often, the visions and goals that we set and chase from a place of ego do not make us happy.

We've all been culturally conditioned to think that we want certain things, particularly in the West. Often these things include wealth, career success, and power. Many people reading this book will have followed a certain path in life up until now, thinking it was what they wanted or what they *should* want. *Should* is a dangerous word but acts as a useful sense-check: if any of your goals in life contain the word *should* then you *should* be very wary of them! I should marry a nice guy from a similar background. I should get a degree. I should plug away at this job I dislike. I should try for promotion. *Should* suggests duty and cultural conditioning. It does not inspire. What about what you *want*?

Before we move on, take a breath. Perhaps close your eyes. Sit in stillness for a moment. Slow down. Don't rush to define what you want. Don't rush into a new life. Think about how far you've come, how much you've achieved, and how many blessings already exist in your life. As Robert Brault said,

 Enjoy the little things, for one day you may look back and realize they were the big things.

WHY WE DON'T KNOW WHAT WE WANT

We're often afraid of having dreams and desires. We've been so busy with our *shoulds*, with duty and diligence. We keep our heads down and plough on with the degree, or with the job that we don't love but which pays the mortgage. As we box ourselves into our life choices, our goals become confined within the parameters of these choices.

When I was in banking, the intensity of the job obliterated all perspective. I was on a treadmill, and my only goals involved how to get further along on that treadmill: how to make Vice President, then Managing Director, then, eventually, Partner (spoiler: the latter two never happened!). There was no real awareness of an outside world, just a general sense of dissatisfaction that I started to feel in my final years in the industry. I was in a bubble, and couldn't see a world beyond it.

Society does a pretty good job of telling us what we should want and how we should value ourselves. We are consumers, and companies need us to stay consumers. It can be incredibly easy to fall into the trap of 'golden handcuffs,' where we upgrade our lifestyle as our salary rises and then get, to some extent, held hostage to that salary. Perhaps our other half is a stay-at-home parent. Perhaps we bought the big house that we thought we *should* have and the kids go to the private school that we were told we *should* get them into. We've valued our success, and set our goals based on these *shoulds* that we've been told we want. No wonder our internal navigation system gets sidelined and we have little faith in our ability to intuit what we really want, especially if it doesn't tally with what society tells us we should want. To revert to Robert Brault's wisdom on this subject:

> We do not knowingly choose unhappiness over happiness. Rather we choose security over risk, stability over change, what seems permanent over what seems fleeting.

We've built ourselves a cocoon and it's safe, familiar, and comforting. We're proud of it, we've worked hard for it, and it's what we always thought we wanted. While we quite rationally fear having this cocoon taken away from us, perhaps there's a greater, less conscious fear that we don't dare give voice to. It's the fear that we've gotten it wrong, that the things we've worked to achieve are not what matter in life and that we don't really want them after all. To turn to an old adage, we should be careful what we wish for.

It's perfectly natural, therefore, that we're scared of dreaming; we're fearful of opening ourselves up and being vulnerable to disappointment or to having to start over. We're terrified that we have unplumbed depths. I read somewhere that our potential is so vast that we could never fulfil it all in one lifetime. I concluded the last chapter with a quote from Marianne Williamson's poem, 'Our Deepest Fear.' I recommend reading it in its entirety if you're not familiar with it, but this is how it opens:

> Our deepest fear is not that we are inadequate.

Our deepest fear is that we are powerful
beyond measure.
It is our light, not our darkness
That most frightens us.

This, then, is why we don't know what we really want in
life. We've always been scared of opening Pandora's box and
unleashing the demons that may taunt us with visions of the
life unlived. And so we've stayed cocooned, choosing not to
search our soul, not to articulate to ourselves our highest
purpose and deepest desires, opting to ignore our true
power.

IDENTIFYING WHAT WE DON'T WANT

When we take steps to define what we want, it can feel as if
we're tying ourselves down to a certain set of outcomes.
There is, as I suggested above, a vast array of options in front
of us, a veritable smorgasbord of human potential. How to
choose which of these paths to follow?

On the other hand, by identifying what we *don't* want,
we can gradually narrow the funnel of our focus. One
benefit of doing this is that a more vivid picture will start to
emerge, in increments, of what we do actually want. But
more practically, establishing what we don't will make our
quality of life far greater. Whether it's the current pain-
points that we're no longer willing to suffer, or future troubles that we're keen to avoid, aligning ourselves so that we
minimise these woes should eradicate a good deal of stress
from our life.

Let's take current pain-points. Whether it's conflict in a
personal relationship, a painful commute, or a job that
makes us miserable, there are many sources of aggravation

that we either need to change or make peace with. As Eckhardt Tolle said:

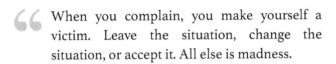 When you complain, you make yourself a victim. Leave the situation, change the situation, or accept it. All else is madness.

When we use the skills learnt in Chapter 2 to start taking responsibility for our troubles, we can accept that our pain-points exist and take ownership of either making them go away or living with them.

Constructing our life to avoid future pain-points is a long-term investment that can yield great dividends. In Chapter 5, we examined the non-negotiables around our health. We can take steps today to ensure that our body will age well into the future. Similarly, we pay down mortgages and invest in our pensions with little benefit now, to ensure peace of mind in later years.

These are the basics of our investments in our future. However, we can take a far bigger-picture view of what we don't want in our future and use this as a springboard for our current choices. I, for example, don't want to stagnate. I don't want to waste my potential. I don't want to look back from my deathbed and think 'what a waste.' I don't want to have shrunk from opportunities because I was scared. It's this definition of my non-negotiables that keeps me moving forward.

This is a good moment for us to tap into the inner wells of wisdom that we discussed in Chapter 4. Remember the letter from your eighty-five-year-old self, where you shared a roadmap to your hopes and dreams and highlighted the extent of your potential? Not only is this exercise a great method for working out what you really want in life, but it can also be a powerful way to understand what you don't want. What if the older self who wrote to you was tired, disillusioned, and full of resentments at your wasted life? What if the letter depicted everything you don't want your life to become?

Charles Dickens famously uses this technique in *A Christmas Carol*. It's not until Scrooge meets The Ghost of Christmas Yet to Come that he fully understands the future implications of his actions. The clarity of the vision that the ghost presents is a huge wake-up call. He understands exactly what he is not willing to endure in his future, and it galvanises him to change his present behaviour immediately.

WORKING OUT WHAT YOU DO WANT

Spoiler: none of your desires can be *shoulds*! This section is not about your duties to anyone else. We all have quite enough duties and responsibilities as it is. This is about what you want, and what you deserve.

The key to tuning out our duties and tuning into our desires is to shift from left-brain to right-brain thinking. If we keep our left brain engaged then we'll over-analyse and use logic to answer our questions. When we ask ourselves what we want, our left brain will most likely tell us what we think we *should* want.

Instead, we want to mobilize our wonderful, creative right brain and mandate it to conjure up spectacular visions for our future. The key here is to ignore reality, ignore any perceived limitations that you or society have imposed on your potential, and just go all-in Disney. Most Disney movies feature an 'I want' song early on, where a lead character paints a picture of his or her dreams that's so vivid and inspiring that the audience buys into their mission whole-heartedly.

Children are also (as you may have noticed) very good at knowing what they want and asking for it continually until they get it. I frequently nickname my kids Veruca Salt, after the spoilt character from *Willy Wonka and the Chocolate Factory*, whose line, 'I want the world. I want the whole world' pretty much sums her up. However, I have to admire children's total focus on their desires. They believe whole-heartedly that they deserve everything they want.

The aim here is to establish a Disneyesque, childlike sense of awe and excitement about the dazzling wonders that await you in life. As Oprah says, 'When I look into the future, it's so bright it burns my eyes.' This may help to explain Oprah's success: unwavering faith in the richness of experience that lies ahead, despite incredible hardship and tragedy in her early life. What if we allowed ourselves to feel this way? What if we chose to believe that not only will everything turn out ok in our future, but that our destiny is to uncover great happiness, wonderful relationships, and spectacular human experiences?

Here are some ways to start the brainstorming process about what you want and to unlock some of your possible resistance to dreaming big:

Elevate Your Environment

Go somewhere inspiring to do this. Sitting at your desk with your laptop is likely to feel too much like work. Find a bench in a beautiful park. Go for a walk in nature. Treat yourself to a coffee in the lobby of a luxurious hotel. Elevate your surroundings and you'll elevate your whole perspective.

Use Vision Boards

If you are visual, start to create some vision boards to get the creative juices flowing. My coach, Charlotte, had me do this. We know that a picture is worth a thousand words and can often capture the essence of idea perfectly. I have vision boards for everything from dream pool houses, to healthy food, yoga retreats, and even real and fictional female role-models with whom I identify. When I'm feeling low-energy or like an imposter, I look at this mood board and find myself able to model the attitude and behaviour of these women.

Imagine If ...

De-risk the process of pinning down your dreams in your own mind by starting with 'Imagine if ...' and brainstorming on what follows. 'Imagine if' is a powerful opener that gives you permission to fantasize about the dreamiest, least likely scenarios. Imagine if I had a house on Lake Como. Imagine if I found a cure for world hunger. Imagine if I allowed myself to be loved. Dave Allen, author of *Getting Things Done,* says:

 'Wouldn't it be great if' is not a bad way to start thinking about a situation, at least for long enough to have the option of getting an answer.

Write Your Own Fairytale

A similar approach is to write a fairytale about yourself in the third person. This offers you the distance you may need from your current reality and enables you to see this very point in your life, as well as what's gone before, as part of a clear story-arc. Let's see what mine looks like.

'Once upon a time there was a little girl called Sara. She loved drawing and dreamed of being a fashion designer, but when she grew up she became a banker. It was a lot of fun but she worked really hard and was tired all the time. She met a wonderful man and had two beautiful babies. She decided to be brave and follow her dreams. She set up a fashion brand with her best friend, dreamed up the most magical dresses and even dressed a real-life princess. Then things got tough and she decided to shut her company down so that she could chase even bigger dreams. She wrote her first book and poured all of the ideas that were in her head onto the page ...'

I won't spoil the ending for you! But you can see that by summarizing your life in a fanciful way, you can unleash the power of limitless thinking and dream up the most magical fate for your protagonist, a fate worthy of a fairytale. The act of writing in this way makes me feel more compassionate towards and protective of myself and my dreams; I feel less likely to judge myself or my ambitions in this scenario than I might otherwise do.

Visualise Yourself Five Years On

I often listen to a beautiful visualisation meditation called 'Your Ideal Life' by Jason Stephenson on YouTube, in which you visualise meeting your future self, five years on, and you have the chance to see yourself in action and to ask yourself questions. I always approached these visualisation exercises with a very clear image of who, what, and where I wanted to be in five years' time, but it's also a great activity if you don't know exactly what you want out of life.

You can replicate this kind of visualisation yourself. After focusing on your breath for a few minutes to centre yourself and find silence, choose an environment for a meeting with your future self, five years on. Here are some questions you can ask yourself:

- What are the main things I notice about my future self?
- What emotional state am I in?
- What level of health do I enjoy?
- Do I have a career? If so, what am I doing in five years' time? If not, what is my focus in life?
- Where am I based?
- Who are the important people in my life?
- What advice does my future self have for me?
- What is my future self most excited about?
- What steps can I take now to pull me towards my future?
- What current facets of my life will not serve me going forward?
- What does my future self tell me not to fear?

I've met with my future self many times and what always strikes me is that she is fearless and serene, two words I would not use to describe myself right now! I am in awe of my future self. She seems comfortable in her own skin in a way that I am not, she's in the flow and is living life fully. The greatest lesson she can teach me is to show me the path to this way of living.

FACTORS TO CONSIDER

What You Want Will, and Should, Change

No one is trying to pin you down here. You have complete freedom to evolve your dreams and goals as you yourself change and develop. Carl Jung coined his Four Stages of Life to define who we are as people. He noted that our motivations will change as we age, 'for what was great in the morning will be little at evening and what in the morning was true, at evening will have become a lie.'

Jung's Four Stages are the Athlete, when we're obsessed by ourselves and our physical appearance; the Warrior, when we become goal-oriented and seek world domination; The Statement, which often coincides with parenthood and where we shift to serving others and finding greater purpose; and The Spirit, where our self-identity rises above our physical form and possessions to focus on what awaits us after we leave our body.

I've always loved the idea of the Four Stages, as it gives me confidence that if we last until old age, we'll have had time to make the mental and spiritual shift that makes our passing feel like the natural next step. It also illustrates how profoundly our desires can change as we mature through these phases. At a simplistic level, we can conclude that we're motivated initially by physical beauty and finding mates, then by money and power, and later by human connection and service, which in turn provide the necessary spiritual growth to evolve to a greater awareness of ourselves as infinite beings.

With these archetypes, Jung essentially lays out humankind's beautiful and continuous metamorphosis, the lifelong hero's journey to be our best and most enlightened selves. If we hold onto desires that we thought we wanted when we were less evolved, then we're doing ourselves a disservice. It's not weakness to acknowledge a shift in our spirituality, belief systems, goals, or dreams; on the contrary, it's a terrible waste of our precious life to hold onto models that no longer service us. It's not fickleness; it's called growth.

Know then, that you can dream up whatever visions you want, revel in them, and swap them out for bigger or completely different dreams whenever you want. It's your life – take as many blank canvasses as you need.

No Shoulds

It's worth re-emphasising this point. In *The Code of the Extraordinary Mind*, Vishen Lakhiani notes that goals are often *shoulds* in disguise. Finishing medical school or bringing home your best-ever bonus: they're either things you think you should do for other people in your life or things you think you should want.

Lakhiani has a brilliant rule of thumb to assess the validity of your goals. He differentiates between means goals and end goals. Often goals are just a means to an end – that medical degree is a means to becoming a doctor. Wanting to help sick and dying people is an end goal. Wanting to be a millionaire, on the other hand, is a means goal. The reason for this is that the money is not an end in yourself; it's a means to being able to afford the things that will please and fulfil you. What you may really want is incredible human experiences. The point is that there are often other ways around the means goals, to get to what your real end goal is. Lakhiani says that end goals are often a feeling:

End goals speak to your soul. They bring you joy in and of themselves, not because they confer any outward label, standard, or value attached by society.

Don't let society dictate what you think you should want.

Skills not Context

This is something I've learnt over the last two decades. I've mentioned that I always wanted to be a fashion designer, and spending eight years creating and running my own brand was an incredible adventure. However, the fashion industry is far less glamorous than it looks from the outside, and the headaches that come with manufacturing and selling a physical product cannot be imagined. While the idea of the fashion industry may sound enticing, the daily grind is far less rewarding.

There were many amazing moments and creative highs running my label, and the sense of satisfaction our team gained from bringing an idea from paper to reality was immense. After a decade of stockbroking, which has always felt to me to be smoke and mirrors, I loved the tangible aspect of fashion. However, I slowly worked out that a huge proportion of what I was doing on a daily basis – essentially managing cashflow, projects, and supply chains – was work that gave me no joy and to which my skill-set is not naturally suited.

Using our talents and developing skills bring us true happiness. Sir Ken Robinson named his book *The Element*, based on the idea that we find our element, or self-fulfilment, through the intersection of our talents and passions. I was not talented at, or passionate about, a large part of the work needed to produce a physical product.

However, as I started to blog more within the context of my company and to read and write more widely beyond that industry, I came to realise something. The things I enjoyed doing were exactly the same as they had been throughout my school years, my history degree and master's, and my career in stockbroking. I named them my Four C's; they're passions and talents that I've nurtured in so many guises, and they put me into a flow state and bring me great pleasure.

They are:

Consuming information. I'm relentless. I read several books a week and listen to podcasts whenever I can. There are such great riches out there and I'm on a mission to read my way to enlightenment! I'm a magpie for ideas.

Connecting the dots between diverse data and concepts and presenting ideas in a new way. I've done this in the contexts of Tudor history, stock-picking, pulling together the details of a dress, and writing this book. My brain gets turned on by 'aha' moments.

Creating, in so many forms. I feel bad for my parents when I look back at my teenage years. Our kitchen was always covered with my experiments, from silk painting and pyrography (wood burning) to batik and clay. While I adored the creativity of building a fashion brand from scratch, these days I prefer the purity of creating through the medium of words. There is no barrier between my thoughts and the paper.

Communicating, distilling, and synthesizing. I love to take myriad inputs and transform them to be more than the sum of their parts. Moreover, I adore sharing nuggets, soundbites, and jewels of wisdom that I have learnt, and packaging them in a fresh way so that they can reach someone who needs them and speak to their soul. Communication is a two-way street and a cornerstone of the human connection that I'm seeking.

Having defined my Four C's, I've become diligent about ensuring that the majority of my time is carved up between these functions. This book is a glorious mash-up of all four and is the ultimate self-indulgence. I'm not entirely sure what the future holds for me, but I know that I want to build a career where I have good reason to keep consuming, and where I can create value by connecting the dots and communicating those findings through my blog, social media, more books, and events where I can connect in person.

When are you at your happiest? Can you see any patterns in your life where you've consistently gravitated towards particular skill-sets, even in widely varied contexts? If so, these patterns may hold the key to finding your element, to unlocking that sacred place where your passions and talents combine and you can make magic. I believe that making it a priority to be in your element, whether through your career or your hobbies, is so important for your health and happiness. Your element could be getting lost in data analysis or cooking for your family.

Take some time to identify the acts that make you happiest and most fulfilled. Then think about how you can incorporate these activities more fully into daily life. It may be that your version of my Four C's are, like mine, very transferrable between different contexts. If so, this is great news. It means not only that you can find a wide variety of ways to indulge in them, but that you can assign them to new contexts if you feel you need a change of career or of lifestyle.

IKIGAI: FINDING MEANING AND PURPOSE

Sir Ken Robinson's idea of the element is closely aligned with the ancient Japanese philosophy of Ikigai, which essentially means 'reason for being.' It's a framework to help us identify that elusive holy grail: our life's purpose. Ikigai is the intersection of four factors which together bring meaning to our life:

1. What you are good at.
2. What you love.
3. What the world needs.
4. What you can be paid for.

If we omit any one of these four elements, we won't achieve the sense of fulfilment that we crave. Together, they provide us with passion, security, satisfaction, and comfort. Ikigai also eases the tension that many of us feel between seeking to make a difference in the world on the one hand, and enjoying a life of financial freedom on the other. While it's intended to portray life as a whole, it may not be reflected in each individual aspect of our life. It's unlikely that we're all going to choose to run social enterprises. Instead, we can choose to find our balance through different silos in life. We may be very good at our job and well rewarded for it; we may seek to enjoy our passions through our hobbies and our service to the world through charity work or caring for our families. That's ok. All of these aspects can come together, reflecting the different parts that make us who we are and bringing harmony to our life.

USING OUR VALUES AS OUR NORTH STAR

What Are Values, and What Are My Values?

It's hard to live a life of meaning and purpose if we don't live according to our values. And it's hard to live according to our values if we have no idea what they are.

Our values are simply what we value: what is most important to us in life. It follows that if we are clear on what's most important to us, and prioritise that at every turn, we're more likely to feel purposeful, on-track, and fulfilled. The problem is that rather than creating our values, we've absorbed most of them from family, society, and figures of influence in our lives.

I did my first exercise around identifying my values with my coach, Charlotte. She gave me a long list of words and asked me to select my top ten values in descending order. In the end, I organised many similar words into groups and came up with ten groups. In total, I had close to ninety values! That's hard to live by.

My struggles were twofold: I wasn't convinced what my values should be, and I had several values that I was pretty sure played a big role in directing my life but which I didn't think served me that well. Should my values list reflect the values I wanted to embody or the values I already embodied? Similar to the paralysis we feel when we're asked to articulate exactly what we want in life, being asked to identify the values that will define our life's journey feels like being a deer caught in the headlights.

Enter the experts. The two teachers whose work on values have been of greatest help to me are Tony Robbins and Brené Brown. Let's take a look at their thoughts on values and what this means for us.

The Experts on Values

I've already cited *Awaken the Giant Within* by Tony Robbins. This is an incredible book that yielded me so many aha moments. I highly recommend his chapter on values (Chapter 15 of his book). Robbins explains that we have moving-toward values (emotional states that we'll do the most to attain) and moving-away-from values (emotions we want to avoid, like fear and rejection). The latter are often bigger drivers of our behaviour, as we will do more to avoid pain than to gain pleasure.

Robbins had his own lightbulb moment prior to writing his book, and it was the realisation that you don't have to accept the values that you think drive you currently; you can consciously select or redirect both your values and the order in which you prioritise them. This is a great example of Robbins' belief that we're not here to *discover* who we are; we're here to *create* who we want to be. Robbins asked himself:

 What do my values need to be in order to create my ultimate destiny, in order to be the best person I could possibly be, in order to have the largest impact in my lifetime?

Earlier in this book, I cited Hal Elrod's assertion that first we need to become the kind of person we need to be, in order to achieve the success we want. This is the same idea and it's based on neuroplasticity. It's an important part of my book and fits with what we've been working on throughout this journey. We can change so much about ourselves, including what drives us; it's part of the work of creating the version of ourselves that we want to be. This is meta-morphosis.

Robbins' words also answered the question I posed to myself at the start of this section. My values should be the values I want to have, rather than the values I think I have. This clarity provided the foundation for me to select the right values for me. My approach has been slightly different from his in that I haven't chosen the values necessary for me to have impact, but rather those that will allow me to live the happiest and most fulfilled life that I can. The essence is the same; we want to choose the values that will make us the best, most fully evolved, version of ourselves.

While Robbins advocates selecting a list of values and being very deliberate about the order in which you place them (for example, putting freedom ahead of family is likely to cause conflict in your family life), Brené Brown takes a more draconian approach and advocates picking only two core values. Bear in mind, she's writing this in *Dare to Lead*, which is ostensibly a book on leadership. But her point is that our core values transcend context; they need to be the same for our personal and professional lives. She says:

Our values should be so crystallized in our minds, so infallible, so precise and clear and unassailable, that they don't feel like a choice – they are simply a definition of who we are in our lives.

Brown's reasons for picking only two core values are that firstly, any more than that and we can't prioritise them effectively, and secondly, we only really need two because these two are where all our 'second tier values' are tested. We'll dive deeper into what she means here when we take a look at my own values in a moment.

Taking the High Road

Essentially, the way to think about values is this: the values we choose define us and our life choices from a high level right down to our tiny, daily decisions. When we act in alignment with our values it should (eventually!) feel great. *However*, most often, acting in accordance with our values is not the easy option; it's usually really, really hard.

Tony Robbins noted that if we have trouble making a decision, then we're not clear on our values. Brown seconds this; her quote above says that our values should make our choices crystal-clear. The distinction is this: values make our decisions easy because they tell us exactly which path to take. However, they make actioning those decisions difficult because usually they dictate that we take the high road, the tougher path: they align with our highest selves and are painful for our ego. As Brown famously puts it, they require us to choose 'courage over comfort.' I've entitled this section 'Using Our Values as Our North Star,' but honestly, more often my values feel like a cattle-prod!

My Values

About a year ago, having benefited from the wise words of Robbins, Brown, and others, and finally armed with a decent idea of what my values are supposed to do for me, I decided to whittle down my list of values. It was so hard! There are so many good ones. In the end, I decided against obvious ones like health, family, and kindness. For me, all those are non-negotiable and a given. The two values that I chose were:

GRATITUDE

HUMAN CONNECTION

I chose these because they're worthwhile, and they're hard. I know that living according to these values will enable me to be happy, fulfilled, and reassured that I'm showing up fully in life as my highest self. I know that I'll reap extraordinary rewards by following them. However, I have historically found them both to be a strain. They haven't come naturally. While intellectually I know that they're worthy values, leaning into them can be a pain in the ass. Choosing to engage with my value of human connection, in particular, is particularly tough.

Here's the interesting thing. Last year, in 2019, I chose gratitude as my word of the year. It was the value that I wanted to live by the most. Writing this, I realise that gratitude is no longer such a strain for me; in fact, it's a natural state and has impacted my life positively in so many ways. I've written about the benefits of gratitude at length in Chapter 7. Do you recall that we also discussed the idea in Chapter 3 that new habits require great discipline, but that when they become habitual they grow effortless, and we can then switch our willpower capacity to embrace a new habit? It appears that this is what's happened to me over the last year. Gratitude has become habitual, and perhaps now's a good time for me to add in a new value and expend my willpower on that. My word for 2020 is surrender. That's going to need some work!

Meanwhile, human connection continues to be a big one for me. I know it's the right value to focus on because it comes up almost daily in the choices I make. I devoted the last chapter to the incredible connections that I believe exist between us all, and yet, at a micro level I find choosing human connection to be tough almost every time. Critically, every single time that I do choose it, I am filled with wonderful blessings and I'm so grateful that I made the right choice. Every time I choose it, I grow. Every time I choose comfort over courage, it leaves a bad taste and I know I've squandered an opportunity to have a meaningful human experience.

Let's look at this one in practice. The opportunity to connect with our fellow humans can take so many forms; there are so many *Sliding Doors* moments every day when we either can show up or pass. These include putting down whatever we're doing and saying yes when our child asks us to play with them, reaching across the bed for our partner when we just want to crash out, stopping to talk to a neighbour or a homeless person, and picking up the phone to call the people we love. I can't think of a single one of these instances when I've regretted my decision to engage, and I almost always regret my decision not to engage.

It may sound as though I bring some consciousness to my human connections but it's amazing how big our blind spots can be! Recently I've been called out on a couple of occasions for not showing up for people I love. To some extent I've been unaware of the impact my behaviour has had on others, but deep-down I knew that I wasn't living according to my values in these cases. I was incredibly grateful to have my ass kicked so that I could make amends and prioritise this value that is so important to me.

When I'm living according to my values, I'm in alignment with my highest self and with my internal compass. This makes me happy and calm and it also aligns me with the universe. We'll talk more in Chapter 11 about why this is so important.

LIFE IS SHORT. WORK OUT WHAT MAKES YOU HAPPY AND GO FOR IT

In her book, *The Top Five Regrets of the Dying*, palliative care nurse Bronnie Ware chronicled the heartbreak that our unlived life can cause us on our deathbeds. Two of the most common regrets of the dying are not having had the courage to live a life true to themselves (as opposed to what others expected) and wishing that they had let themselves be happier. Ware says: 'This is a surprisingly common one. Many did not realise until the end that happiness is a choice.'

I believe happiness is a choice and a state of being. We can't find it wrapped up in a new car or a promotion. It's not a destination. It's not conditional. When we're true to ourselves and we know what we want from life, we're more likely to get it, and we're more likely to find happiness and fulfilment. We owe it to ourselves to put in the time and work to figure out what we want. The final two chapters are about making it happen for ourselves.

You can check out my favourite books and other resources for What Do We Actually Want From Life? at www.healthywealthyandwiseuk.com/met

10

IT'S NOT LUCK, IT'S SYNCHRONICITY

*At various points in our lives, or on a quest, and for reasons that
often remain obscure, we are driven to make decisions which
prove with hindsight to be loaded with meaning.*

Sri S. Satchidananda

One Saturday afternoon in the summer of 2007, I called my
colleague, Jo. She had been in hospital the previous day and
I was keen to see how she was doing, and to ask if she would
like me to come over and keep her company. Jo thanked me
but explained that her brother had called round with his
friend and that she was in good hands. Unbeknownst to me,
after Jo had hung up, her brother's newly-single friend said
to her, 'You must have a nice friend that you can set me up
with.' Because she'd just spoken to me, I was at the front of
her mind. She suggested that we get in touch.

The guy duly contacted me and we agreed to go on a
blind date. When we were discussing where we should go, it

transpired that we lived less than five hundred metres away from each other (this is in a city of ten million people). I, in fact, lived on a little mews that ran off his street. We both had the same flat number – 15A – and we shared the same postcode aside from the last digit. It also turned out that we had occasionally received each other's post over the previous months, and continued to do so as we dated.

As Jane Eyre would say, 'Reader, I married him.' Jo's brother's friend, Chris, became my husband, and I have never looked back since that blind date. For years afterwards, I tortured myself with the tenuous nature of our introduction. There were so many what-ifs. What if I hadn't called Jo that day? What if Chris hadn't visited her? What if I'd declined the set-up (I was pretty disillusioned with blind dates by then)? How could I marry (pun intended) the gravitas of meeting the single most important person in my life with the fact that our meeting could easily have never happened? I couldn't believe I had got so lucky.

THE WORKINGS OF SYNCHRONICITY

I mentioned the movie *Sliding Doors* in the last chapter; being set up with Chris felt like one of those *Sliding Doors* experiences where our entire future is decided in the flip of a coin. However, after several years of getting conscious, growing, and settling into a spirituality that works for me, I have a very different take on the forces that brought about our union. Rather than random 'good fortune,' I believe that my soulmate and I were always meant to be together, and discovered each other thanks to the glorious machinations of the universe. In other words, it wasn't luck, it was synchronicity.

Let me take my beliefs a step further. Laura Lynne Jackson's beautiful work on the interconnectedness we share with each other and with those who have crossed has impacted me so much. Jackson's view is that our 'team of light' – loving spirit guides who look out for us and help us – work with humans here on earth to help them achieve their wonderful plans for us. When the departed work through us, we are acting as connectors. I love to think that there was a vast team of light pulling celestial strings to unite Chris and me. And the fact that Jo is responsible for setting up several other married couples too tells me that the Other Side values her as a connector!

I've mentioned a few of my core beliefs and philosophies in the preceding chapters. I've told you that I choose to live as though the universe is a friendly place and as though everything is a miracle. I've also shared my mantra, or master key, which is 'everything is unfolding precisely as it should.' All of these foundational beliefs lead me to favour synchronicity over luck. We've discussed our freedom to select the models of reality that serve us best, and I find that believing that our lives are flawlessly synchronised as part of a beautiful universal dance, is a model that serves me far better than assuming that life plays out in a meaningless, random way.

Synchronicity is a term coined by Carl Jung to describe meaningful coincidences. It's worth noting that the term 'coincidence,' when used in a mathematical context, means 'to fit together perfectly.' Coincidence here means coinciding angles or lines sitting exactly on top of one another. Jung saw synchronicity as related events brought together by meaning, rather than by any causal relationship.

Synchronicity is really a part of a bigger belief system. Embracing synchronicity is a statement that you believe we're not all here by chance; we are not here to simply survive as long as we can before we return to dust. It's a statement that you see meaning and form in the way that the universe is composed, that you buy into the interconnectedness of all things on this planet, and that your life has purpose. It's an act of faith in the idea that there are greater forces at work, that you are not alone, and that, as Gabby Bernstein so reassuringly puts it, 'the universe has your back.'

I believe that there are far too many meaningful coincidences in life to ascribe them to luck or random chance. When serendipitous moments occur, I find them magical! To me they're like winks from the universe. Another term I've heard is divine breadcrumbs, tiny cosmic clues that reassure us that we're on the right path. I keep a list on Evernote of the divine breadcrumbs that come my way.

Here are a couple of examples:

I was in the hairdresser's when I had a call to say my close friend's husband had died. Needless to say, I was beside myself. Moments later, a song came on the radio. It was Aretha Franklin's 'You're All I Need to Get By,' the song Chris and I had our first dance to at our wedding. I took it as a sign from the universe that it was looking out for us as a couple, and it gave me some comfort in the moment.

Another example: a few years ago, we had taken the decision to exit our brand's wholesale business but I had an outstanding meeting in the diary with a large wholesale partner in Berlin. The day before I had to fly out there, I was racking my brains for an excuse to cancel the meeting. I knew it would be a complete waste of everyone's time if I went. That evening, I had a call from Chris to say he was launching a deal the next morning and had to leave the house at 5am to get into the office on time – he wouldn't be able to do the morning shift with the kids or the school drop-off; I'd have to cancel my trip. My response? Awesome!

I know that believing in synchronicity can be a big leap of faith because of the implications of that belief. You're essentially buying into a whole eco-system of quantum-physics-based spirituality. But sometimes it's worth taking a flutter outside of your cocoon, beyond the familiarity of your constructs, to enjoy the magic. And if you've seen *Sliding Doors* you'll remember the ending. After illustrating how a split-second event (making, or missing, the tube as the doors were closing) could send Helen's life spiralling in two completely different possible directions, she ended up in the same place anyway. She met James. Some things are just written in the stars.

WE CAN'T TELL GOOD LUCK FROM BAD LUCK

When we discussed judgement in Chapter 8, I mentioned that we not only judge others, but we permanently judge situations. It turns out, we really have no authority, let alone sufficient perspective, to judge whether situations are good or bad. You may have heard an old Taoist tale about an elderly farmer. I've seen several versions of it so I'll summarise it briefly. One day the farmer's horse ran away. 'Such bad luck,' the villagers commented. 'Maybe,' he replied. Then the horse returned with three wild horses. The villagers thought this was great luck. Again, the farmer replied: 'Maybe.' The farmer's son then broke his leg riding one of the wild horses. The villagers saw this as such a misfortune, but the farmer's response was, as usual, 'Maybe.' Soon after, the military arrived to draft young men of the village into the army, but the farmer's son was passed over due to his broken leg. You can imagine what the farmer's response was.

This story serves to show that while we all tend to have knee-jerk reactions, we are ill-equipped to judge whether events or situations are really 'good' or 'bad.' We lack many perspectives, especially the perspective of time. One of the best soundbites I've come across recently is from Gabby Bernstein in *Super Attractor*: 'Rejection is protection.' I think this is brilliant. Often, when the universe delivers what seems to be a blow, it is protecting us from an even bigger blow down the road. It turns out that a broken leg beats military conscription.

I was reading Julie Andrews' autobiography, *Home Work*, recently, and she recalled how devastated she was to have been passed over for the role of Eliza Doolittle in the movie version of *My Fair Lady*, having played the role on Broadway. Had she bagged the role, she wouldn't have been available to work on *Mary Poppins*, which won her an Oscar and worldwide fame. Andrews tells us how, in her final weeks of shooting *Mary Poppins*, she was driving past the Warner Bros. Studio. *My Fair Lady* had just started shooting there. She yelled out, 'Thank you *very* much, Mr Warner!' Sometimes, we just need to get out of own way, stop judging everything and trust that the universe knows exactly what it's doing.

WE MAKE OUR OWN LUCK

Whether or not you buy into my beliefs of universal synchronicity, there's one thing I know to be true. We make our own luck, both good and bad. The type of 'luck' that we generate for ourselves is closely related to our ability to take responsibility for everything that happens in our life. People who consider themselves unlucky tend to have a victim mentality; life happens *to* them, not *for* them. Lucky people, on the other hand, can otherwise be described as self-responsible; they accept and own their circumstances.

I've mentioned Sir Ken Robinson, author of *The Element* and one of the most watched TED Talk speakers of all time. Robinson attributes luck to our attitude. In *The Element*, he observes that as well as aptitude, you must have the right approach to achieve any degree of success:

> Good and bad things happen to all of us. It's not what happens to us that makes the difference in our lives. What makes the difference is our attitude toward what happens.

I would define making our own luck in the following terms: firstly, taking one hundred percent responsibility for our circumstances; secondly, not judging what happens to us as 'good' or 'bad'; thirdly, asking why things are happening *for* us rather than *to* us; and fourthly, keeping our eyes open for signs that synchronicity is at work. People who deem themselves to be unlucky may be overlooking opportunities that people who make their own luck are open to.

Robinson cites a study by psychologist Dr Richard Wiseman, who set up an experiment which involved planting a five-pound note outside a cafe. Someone who believed himself to be 'lucky' was sent into the shop, found the money, used it to buy a coffee for himself and the person sitting next to him in the café, and struck up a lovely conversation. Another volunteer, self-diagnosed as 'unlucky,' missed the money completely. I mean...! This goes right to

Robinson's point. The exact same 'luck' factors were at play for both parties here. The differentiator was their attitudes.

Before I leave Robinson's wonderful book (which I highly recommend, especially if you have school-age children), I want to share another quote. Robinson writes, 'One way of opening ourselves up to new opportunities is to make conscious efforts to look differently at our ordinary situation.' This comes back to Chapter 7 of this book, 'Perception is Reality.' Luck is all around us. It's how you view it that matters. We can live as though everything, or nothing, is a miracle, as though we're the most fortunate person in the world or the most jinxed. Whichever we believe will be our reality.

We're nearing the end of this stage in our journey, discovering the incredible wonders that lie all around us in plain sight. Soon we'll be ready to take flight. This short chapter has set the scene for the final step, which is more like a super-power: the capacity to connect into the flow of this synchronicity and manifest what we desire into our life.

You can check out my favourite books and other resources for It's Not Luck, it's Synchronicity at
www.healthywealthyandwiseuk.com/met

11

MANIFESTATION, DECODED

I just want to share my belief in the incredible power of manifesting—the harnessing, owning, and directing of our energy to create a future that is worthy of us.

Laura Lynne Jackson

This is what it all comes down to: our ability to manifest into our reality that which we desire. Manifesting, and the law of attraction, have become ubiquitous concepts in the spiritual and personal growth arenas, and books such as Rhonda Byrne's *The Secret* have helped to foster the idea of manifesting as a shortcut, a way to get rich quick by mocking up a million-dollar bill, sticking it on your bathroom mirror, and looking at it while you brush your teeth every day. Perhaps that's unfair, but I do think the art of manifesting is hard for us laypeople to get our heads around, and so it's worth taking a proper look at what it involves.

This final chapter is a reminder that I'm right alongside you on this journey. I'm no master manifestor; it's an area that I find intriguing but confusing and, above all, frustrating. Manifestation is a slippery concept and there are so much conflicting pieces of information out there, as well as a lot of cowboys.

I do, however, know this much. Given what I understand about our interconnectedness, the laws of quantum physics, and the synchronicity with which our universe works, I find manifestation, and the law of attraction, to be concepts that I can definitely believe in. I also think they present a plausible explanation for why some people can effortlessly attract abundance and joy, while others are stuck in cycles of scarcity and pain.

If we can master the art of manifesting everything that we dream of and yearn for, it will be the key to a life of abundance and wonder. To that end, I've done what I love to do. I've consumed the work of many great teachers in this sphere, making connections and drawing patterns in my mind, and weighing up how valid and helpful their theories and practices are. The result: six steps that paint a picture of how we may attain this holy grail. But before we kick off, let's examine the foundations of the law of attraction, which holds the basis for our ability to manifest.

THE LAW OF ATTRACTION, AND MANIFESTING

If you're less familiar with the law of attraction, it's the theory that we each attract the conditions and experiences of our life through our own thoughts and emotions, whether or not we're aware of doing so. The law of attraction is understood to be as universal as gravity: it knows no exceptions. The concept has been around in some form since the end of the nineteenth century, but the discovery of quantum physics has galvanised its adoption by providing a scientific explanation for how it works.

The law goes like this: we are all energy, and we vibrate at different frequencies depending on our emotional state (we know that elevated emotions such as love, joy, and gratitude have a high frequency, and base emotions like shame and despair have a low frequency. We can raise, or improve, our frequencies by elevating our emotional state and thinking positive thoughts. The law of attraction says that like attracts like. If we have negative thoughts and emotions, we attract more of the same. If we approach life from a place of scarcity, we'll attract more scarcity to our lives. If we live abundantly and think abundant thoughts, we'll attract only abundance.

The principle of manifesting, therefore, is based on the idea that we can harness the law of attraction by deliberately choosing our visions, thoughts, and emotions, and making these a reality by matching the energy of these thoughts to the energy of what we desire: in other words, making a vibrational match. As Dr Wayne Dyer puts it, we can use this energy because we are energy. Gabby Bernstein, another author whose work on manifesting has been very inspiring to me, says in *Super Attractor*:

Manifesting is the creative process of aligning with the energy of the Universe to co-create an experience that elevates your spirit and the spirit of the world. Manifesting isn't about getting; it's about becoming.

This harks back to Hal Elrod's view that we must become who we need to be before we can get what we want. Once we metamorphose sufficiently, we are empowered to co-create whatever we want in life. Bernstein's use of the word 'aligning' is also key. To manifest is essentially to tap into our interconnectedness, to the universal stream of creation of which we're a part.

One of my all-time favourite books is *The Power of Intention* by Dr Wayne Dyer. It's the only book that I own in paper, audio, and e-book format! Dyer explains that he had always thought of intention as something that comes from us. For him, it was always about our mindset; we could intend something into being by sheer force of will. He happened upon some work by Carlos Castaneda that caused him to overturn all his beliefs. Castaneda's words were,

> Intent is a force that exists in the universe. When sorcerers [Dyer's note: those who live of the source] beckon intent, it comes to them and sets up the path for attainment, which means that sorcerers always accomplish what they set out to do.

This caused Dyer to understand that intention doesn't have to mean striving tirelessly, but that instead it exists as a field of energy and that we can access it effortlessly. That's what we're going to set out to do.

The six steps that I've identified are as follows:
1. Visualise
2. Live from the End
3. Positive Emotion
4. Surrender
5. Unwavering Faith & Infinite Patience
6. Take Aligned Action

Let's look at these in detail.

1. VISUALISE

Abraham-Hicks is a collective term for authors Jerry and Esther Hicks, as well as Abraham, which describes itself as 'a group consciousness from the non-physical dimension'. The Hicks have conversed with Abraham for decades, using Esther as a channel. They observe in *The Law of Attraction* that the problem for humankind is that we spend most of our time focused on 'what is' – namely our current situations. We therefore attract more of what is. When we do think about the future, it's often in a state of worrying. We then attract what we don't want. If we spend our days mired in mainly mediocrity or negativity, it's no wonder that this is what we continue to attract into our lives.

Visualisation is a wonderful gift, unique to humans. We can see things that do not exist, as if they do. We owe all of our cultural, societal, and technological advances to men and women who've harnessed the power of their imaginations. As George Bernard Shaw's benign serpent in "Back to Methuselah" says, 'I dream things that never were; and I say "Why not?"'

Visualisation should be *fun;* it should be gloriously self-indulgent and the ultimate treat to luxuriate in our thoughts. Many of us don't do it enough because, as we covered in Chapter 9, we're not sure what we really want. If you're still struggling with that, Abraham-Hicks suggest stating first of all when meditating or sitting quietly, 'I want to know what I want.' They see life as a beautiful scrapbooking exercise, where we can go about collecting data on what we do and don't want, and building a wonderful montage of our wildest dreams.

Get Your Limiting Beliefs Out of The Way

Many of us feel blocked when we try to visualise what we want from life. We feel unworthy. We don't love ourselves sufficiently. We fear that the world is binary, and that abundance for me means scarcity for others. We feel selfish wanting more when we already have so much. We've been warned off by Icarus' fate: don't dream too big. Don't expect too much of yourself. Don't fly too close to the sun. Keep your head down. But as we established in Chapter 1, if you're reading this book, mediocrity is not something you're going to settle for.

There's nothing wrong with wanting to grow, to achieve, to make a difference to others, and to feel as though we've lived a big life. Even the Bible tells us to go for it:

 Ask, and it shall be given you; seek, and ye shall find; knock, and it shall be opened unto you:

For every one that asketh receiveth; and he that seeketh findeth; and to him that knocketh it shall be opened. (Matthew 7: 7-8)

Get Creative

Taking 15-20 minutes out of your day to indulge in some visualisation is a beautiful thing. First, take a moment to revisit the 'Working Out What You Do Want' section in Chapter 9. The techniques listed there will help to get your right-brain fired up. Think of one thing that you really desire, and imagine yourself already in that state. It could be enjoying your dream villa, or receiving your promotion, or imagining your family healthy and happy, one generation on from now, at a big family event.

The key here is to get specific, and try to fill in as many details as possible. This really brings the image to life. For example, if you're imagining your dream retreat in the south of France, act out a scene in your head. Perhaps it's early morning and you're doing laps in your pool while the sun comes up on the Côte d'Azur. Perhaps you're enjoying a lazy Mediterranean feast for lunch on the terrace. What would you smell, taste, see, and hear? Most importantly, how would you *feel*? Bringing elevated emotions into the visualisation is key. Revel in it!

Another seriously enjoyable way to visualise is to run through your perfect day in your head. Get relaxed, and take yourself through the details. Do you have an incredible power-shower? What's your morning practice? Look at your work life. Imagine how fulfilled and inspired you feel in your dream role.

When I visualise this book being well received, I get very specific. I find that a general idea of its 'success' is too hard to pin down and so I imagine some really detailed scenarios. There are a few podcasts that I would love to be invited on to discuss the book. I visualise myself recording these podcasts, and I imagine everything from what I would wear (you can take the girl out of fashion ...) to what kind of tea I'd be offered, to how the studio would look, to the warm-hearted chat I'd have on- and off-air with some of my favourite podcasters. I can really live these experiences in my mind as though they're happening now. So get granular!

I tend to role-play the scenario in my mind because that's the way my brain works, but you may find that you can more easily visualise a snapshot or observe your vision from a fly-on-the-wall perspective. In this situation, you may want to compose some affirmations to cement in your brain what you are visualising. This works very well if you are writing out your visualisation too. For example, if you're visualising your perfect day, you can affirm how you feel when you wake up ('I awake feeling rested, recharged, and full of excitement for the day ahead'), how you behave at work ('I am a confident, compassionate leader who is deeply committed to nurturing my team') and so forth.

Consistent Focus

Abraham-Hicks make the point that we are all so distracted that it's hard to focus properly on what we really want, so we dilute and weaken our point of attraction to it. The observer effect in quantum physics (whereby particles change their behaviour when we focus on them) and the law of attraction both tell us that you get what you give your attention to, whether you want it or not. Consistently focusing on, returning to, and adding layers of detail to our highest priority desires will strengthen our manifesting power. There is a less spiritual and more pragmatic aspect to the power of focus too. We've talked about our Reticular Activation System. The more attention we bring to a subject, the more prominence that subject gains in our consciousness and the more of it life serves up to us. In this way, what we focus on can become a self-fulfilling prophecy.

2. LIVE FROM THE END

If you're doing what I suggested above, then you're already, in Dr Dyer's words, 'living from the end': in your mind you've already achieved your wildest dreams. You've immersed yourself in your vision and played out your movie in real time. You're behaving as if what you desire has already occurred for you. This is critical in visualisation.

Go Quantum, Not Newtonian

Visualisations need to be imagined as taking place in the present. This is because we're using the quantum field, where time and space do not exist in the way that we think of them, to create.

A Newtonian model involves cause and effect – something happens, so I can then be grateful for it, or enjoy it. A quantum model, as Dr Dispenza explains, means that you put the thought out there first and you are 'causing an effect (changing something inside of you to produce an effect *outside* of you).' Dispenza goes into great detail about the differences between the two models, and the way to harness the quantum model, in *Breaking the Habit of Being Yourself*.

Essentially, we're being asked to do something completely foreign to us: to rely, not on our senses, but on our emotions to make sense of the world. Dyer reassures us that:

 This isn't pretending or fooling yourself, it is inviting your spirit rather than your physical form to generate the creative essence of your reality.

Focus on the Outcome and Ignore the Means

The next step of living from the end is to focus on the 'happy ending' and try not to get bogged down in how this outcome will come about. There are a few reasons for this. Firstly, the quantum field doesn't need it. Dispenza says, 'If you're trying to control how an outcome will occur, you just went "Newtonian."'

Secondly, you'll see shortly that it's important to maintain both an elevated emotional state and a high level of certainty around the outcome of your dreams. Getting yourself stressed about how the universe will conspire to make your dreams a reality impacts both your mood, and your faith that they can be pulled off. Abraham-Hicks suggest getting as specific as you can handle – sometimes specifics will enhance the vividness of your visualisations – but pulling back if the specifics are causing you problems.

Third, the universe works in a seriously cool way! One of the greatest things about seeing how our visions are manifested is that feeling that we couldn't have made it up – we couldn't possibly have foreseen what kind of amazing strings the universe would pull. When I was itching to get out of my wholesale meeting in Berlin, it didn't occur to me that the universe would arrange for Chris to have a work obligation that took away my childcare. Cool solution! Just trust the process. Dyer says that 'if the end is secured, the means is also handled.'

After the Visualisation

Dispenza makes the argument that if we get up from our meditation the same person we were when we sat down, it will have been a fruitless exercise:

 From a quantum standpoint, we have to create a different state of being as an observer and generate a new electromagnetic signature. When we do, we will match a potential reality in the field that exists only as an electromagnetic potential.

In practice, this means getting up and living as though we'd just had our wildest dreams fulfilled, in order to create a vibrational match with those dreams.

3. POSITIVE EMOTION

All of the teachers whom I respect in this field are emphatic about the value of bringing positive emotion to the manifesting experience. Abraham-Hicks believe that its importance is due to the fact that our emotions represent our internal guidance system. When we experience positive emotions, we know that we are acting in accordance with our Inner Being, our higher self who is older and wiser than our physical self. When we feel negative emotions, we know that we're in conflict with our Inner Being. This is significant because our manifesting power comes from this Inner Being, which is in complete alignment with the creative forces of the universe.

Another way of viewing this is that our emotions change our vibrations, and we need to be a vibrational match with the quantum field, or universal power, in order to manifest our desires. The key to effective manifesting is to hold a thought in our head and to experience an elevated emotion alongside that. Dispenza explains that all potential experiences exist as electromagnetic signatures in the quantum field. Our thoughts are an electrical signal out into the field, and our emotions are the magnetic signal that draws these desires back to us. As Dispenza says:

 Together, how we think and how we feel

produces a state of being, which generates an electromagnetic signature that influences every atom in our world.

Gabby Bernstein puts it in a less technical way:

 Focusing on feeling good is much more valuable than focusing on your exact desire or goal. The Universe responds to energy and delivers circumstances and opportunities that are a vibrational match. If your desire feels far from reach, concentrate on what feels good and you'll get closer to your desire.

I Want vs. I Need

I'd always found it difficult to really want something without portraying a sense of scarcity or lack in my visualisations. After all, traditionally the word 'want' means to lack, as in 'I want for a wife,' or I lack a wife. If the universe attracts what we're emitting, then more scarcity seems like an easy thing to attract (and explains a lot about where society is today).

I've found Abraham-Hicks' thoughts on this helpful. They suggest that wanting, as in desiring, is fine as long as it comes from a place of deep enthusiasm and excitement for what we're visualising. If we can be greatly joyful about the baby or the promotion or the good health that we want, then this sends out the right signal to the universe. Neediness, on the other hand, does send a signal of scarcity and should be avoided.

The Power of Appreciation

Gratitude and appreciation are such an important part of the manifestation process. When we express gratitude for an experience before it happens, we are moving from a Newtonian to a quantum model; we're acting as the change agent rather than a passive recipient. So alongside the joy and excitement that you bring to your visualisations, conjure up big helpings of gratitude. Luxuriate in appreciation for what you desire and expect. What we appreciate, we create more of. Appreciate both the things that you love in your life to keep them coming, and the things that are yet to show up on this physical plane.

4. SURRENDER

In Chapter 6, we discussed how easy, and limitless, life can be when we surrender. We covered Bernstein's warnings against using 'pushy' energy, trying to control means and outcomes – essentially, what I've been doing for most of my life. She also calls it 'manic manifesting,' where we exhaust ourselves by wildly using all of our spiritual tools while forgetting to tune into the power of the universe by getting out of our own way and *allowing*. She says, 'Instead of allowing yourself to receive, you want to "get."'

I mentioned earlier, that surrender is one of my keywords for 2020. I'm finding the state of surrender and 'allowing' to be blissful. It reminds me of when I met Chris. I was very independent because I'd had to be; I'd been mostly single for the previous few years and as a home-owner living alone, I'd had to get on with things and look after myself. I remember the first Christmas we were together. Instead of my going out to buy a seven-foot tree and working out how to persuade a cabbie to take me and it home and how to get it set up, Chris took me tree-shopping in his car and set it up for me. It was heaven!

I learnt, quickly, that this amazing man had come into my life and would look after me, whether I needed it or not. I think it's a similar vibe with the universe. I'm so used to trying to push and control all outcomes, that when I realise there's a far easier and more effective solution, I give in gracefully and enjoy the ride. I collapse in gratitude and relief, and know that I'm in safe hands. Because here's the thing. Who are we to think we know what's best for us?

We've already established that we don't have a clue. The intelligence that created us will always have a much bigger and better dream for us than we have for ourselves. The flow of creation feels like a river; we can jump out onto the bank but there, on our own, we're not going to get very far. If we return to the river, we know that we can be carried along on its sense of direction, on its intent.

When we doubt that we can achieve our dreams, it almost always comes from a sense of unworthiness or scarcity. These doubts dilute the power of our visualisations. They undercut the 'belief' side of the equation. When we're dreaming of what may be, rather than what is, we have to find a way to tell our ego to step aside so that we can suspend our disbelief. Our ego's needy, cynical vibes are the quickest way to sabotage our dreams.

Surrendering them to the care of a higher power is the best way to prevent this. As Oprah Winfrey says:

 Don't hold anything too tightly – just wish for it. Want it. Let it come from the intention of real truth for you and then let it go. And if it's supposed to be yours it will show up and it

won't show up until you stop holding it so
tightly.

5. UNWAVERING FAITH & INFINITE PATIENCE

Unwavering Faith

I can visualise till the cows come home. I have a very active
imagination and am a visual person, so visualisation is easy
for me. Where I often struggle, is with the belief side of the
equation. I can too easily go to a place of unworthiness and
scarcity. I love to imagine the experiences that I want, but I
don't realistically think I can get them.

Abraham-Hicks would explain this as resistance to
going beyond 'what-is.' When we're so used to focusing on
what is in plain sight, it's a big leap of faith to imagine that
things can be any other way. But faith is precisely what we
need here. We have to be like a butterfly: untethered, and
undefined by what we were in our past. Dyer explains that
when we're going beyond what we are or used to be, we
need faith in our own power. Our limiting beliefs have no
place here.

Unwavering faith is one half of Hal Elrod's *Miracle Equation*. While Elrod's approach tends more towards the pragmatic than the spiritual, there are many parallels between
his framework for bringing about miracles in our lives and
the philosophy of manifesting. He cautions that:

 there is a potentially devastating downside to
skepticism that we all need to be aware and
cautious of: it can easily turn into cynicism. It
can tip us into an unhealthy level of distrust

and limit the possibilities that are otherwise available to us.

If unworthiness, scarcity and scepticism are the three biggest impediments to our faith in bringing about that which we want, then limitless thinking, an abundance mindset, and an understanding of the workings of the quantum field are the antidotes. Revisit Chapter 6, 'Farewell to Limiting Beliefs ... Welcome to Limitless Living,' should you need a refresher on the possibilities that await us when we make the switch from unworthiness to self-belief. For a detailed understanding of quantum theory, I wholeheartedly recommend Dr Joe Dispenza's work. Thankfully, he has a talent for explaining the technicalities in plain English that even I, emotionally scarred by my secondary school Physics lessons, can understand.

I think that all three blocks to belief or expectation are linked. We don't think we are worthy of more because scarcity is so engrained. Scarcity is engrained because we've done such a great job of manifesting more scarcity throughout our lives, more of 'what is.' We've done this because we haven't properly understood these powerful universal laws. We're sceptical that they work because they sound woo-woo and so unlike the Newtonian model of reality we've been brought up with. But if we see what we've managed to manifest in life so far, and we take an honest inward look at the negative thought and behaviour patterns and victim mindset that many of us have embodied for years, then ironically this is pretty good proof that there might be something to this manifesting lark!

This book is about making the necessary inward changes, before we can make outward changes. The first part of the book focuses inwards. The second part examines our current reality and adjusts our perceptions, before we start to make the big changes in our lives. Up until this point, we've behaved in a certain way and attracted an appropriate reality. Today, we're a different person from the person who picked up this book. We must have faith that we're therefore empowered to manifest a different reality.

Infinite Patience

Faith and patience are inextricably linked. When we have complete faith and we surrender, we have patience because we know that what we want *will* come about. The metaphysical text, *A Course in Miracles*, says 'Infinite patience produces immediate results.' Dr Dyer explains this paradox in the following way: when we know we're in vibrational alignment with the universe, and are indeed co-creating with it, we can know that everything will show up right on time. Trying to rush things is like pulling up a tulip shoot before the flower has had a chance to bloom. Meanwhile, 'the immediate result that you'll receive from your infinite patience is a deep sense of peace.' This comes back to quantum theory. Even if the event hasn't manifested yet, we can enjoy a sense of enjoyment, gratitude, and peace *immediately*. Impatience, on the other hand, is a construct of the ego and implies duality, rather than unity with the forces at work.

Abraham-Hicks have a slightly different take. The law of attraction dictates that the more strongly we desire and believe in a vision, the more quickly it will manifest. So if we're not diluting our visualisations, we shouldn't need patience. However, the value in not rushing our manifestations is that we may need to achieve the right vibration for ourselves before we rush through big changes in our lives. I take this to mean that if we attain huge wealth or success, for example, before we are ready for it, it's harder for us to manage this leap – and to hold onto it. Lottery winners and celebrities who are overnight successes are examples of this scenario.

For me, allowing the universe to take its time in the knowledge that 'everything is unfolding precisely as it should,' is an important part of manifesting. We've agreed that we don't have the perspective to know what is good or bad for us; it follows that neither are we the best judge of *when* we should get what we want. We're here on this earth to learn, and the universe has multiple lessons for us to learn. As we know, getting what we want whenever we want it will not help us to evolve.

6. TAKE ALIGNED ACTION

I've done a good bit of visualising around completing this book, launching it, and watching it be a success. But let's be clear, I still needed to write the book! Manifestation may pave the path for us, but we must walk the path nevertheless. Elrod puts it well at the start of *The Miracle Equation*:

 I began actively moving toward my biggest goals, instead of expecting (more like hoping) that they would come to me if I could just visualize them clearly in my mind.

Yes, the universe works in mysterious and beautiful ways, and loves to surprise and delight us. There is, I guess, some chance that *Metamorphosis* ends up in the hands of Oprah or Ellen and changes my life. But I still need to show up. I still need to write, to edit, to market, and to engage. Just as when things come too quickly to us it can cause problems, when things come too easily and we don't believe that we've earned them, we're unlikely to be able to sustain them. To return to the example of lottery winners, I don't think it's a huge surprise that many of them find that the money brings misery; they burn through their winnings, and return to life as they knew it before. They weren't a perfect vibrational match for this quantum leap that they'd made.

The approach that most of my teachers take is that effective visualisation ignites the spark within us; it inspires us with both a clear vision of what we want, and a firm belief that we can achieve it. It inspires us to take action. When we take action that is *aligned* with the universal source, we will find that doors open up, roads rise up to meet us, and our work bears fruit. Moreover, when we take action from a place of love and joy, we feel great and it doesn't seem like work. This is when we are in our element; we're in the zone, in a flow state. We are purposeful and fulfilled.

Action Gets Us Over the Hurdle From Metaphysical to Physical

One problem with visualising the glory of the 'finish line' is that it may cause us to become overly complacent. We think that if we mock up that million-dollar cheque or pin up a photo of our dream home or an athletic body, that it will somehow just materialise. But we still need to show up for our dreams, and sometimes the fact that we have to put in the work can be a rude awakening.

Maria Nemeth captures this conflict perfectly in her book *The Energy of Money*, with a concept called 'trouble at the border.' She explains that when we are visualising properly, we're in a wonderful state of high vibration and attracting what we desire with ease. When we are ready to take this into the physical plane, however, we encounter resistance because we have to adjust to the fact that this realm has a much denser vibration that requires far more energy. The resistance shows up in the form of doubts, fears, and inertia.

The way that we overcome this resistance and get ourselves over the hurdle is with the right kind of action. We invoke the tools we've learnt so far in this chapter: vivid visualisation, belief, focus, positive emotion, surrender, and faith, and we get to work. Gabby Bernstein says:

 When we merge our desire with our faith, we can take action from a place of peace rather than control. It's this presence of peace that allows the Universe to support us fully.

It's similar to when you're doing a particularly important or difficult project at work. If you know that you have a supervisor who's far more qualified than you watching over you, you can relax and just get on with the job at hand.

IN CONCLUSION

Whatever its perceived shortcomings, the book *The Secret* makes a staggering point. What if we've created every single condition in our life to date, and what if, hiding in plain sight, there's a secret that only the greatest minds know to be true: that we can recreate our experience in whatever way we want, by tapping into the universal source?

The manifesting framework that I've laid out above may sound prescriptive, and that's the last thing I want. One of the things I object to the most about organised religion is its layers of dogma and its insistence upon telling us exactly how we should think and act. I don't want to do the same here. The more I learn, the more fully I believe that life is, at its core, very straightforward. Under all the instructions above lies a simple message: we can align with the source of the universal power that's created us all, and from this place we can co-create. When we have clarity and faith in our ability to do this, we'll find it easy not only to envision the most beautiful future for ourselves, but to surrender all of our hopes and dreams to this incredible power. I believe that when we choose to work with the universal flow, rather than against it, manifesting our dreams is effortless.

You can check out my favourite books and other resources for Manifestation, Decoded at
www.healthywealthyandwiseuk.com/met

AFTERWORD: FLY AWAY

Tell me, what is it you plan to do
with your one wild and precious life?

Mary Oliver

We have one life as this particular person, in this physical reality. That's it. We don't know how many days, or months, or years, we have left. Meanwhile, we bear the cultural, social, and religious hangover of thinking that life should be a struggle; this received wisdom is tattooed onto our consciousness. We've seen millennia of toil, strife, and disease; good people living *hard* lives. The crushing weight of all these influences leaves us unable to breath. It's no surprise that they inform our reality. We use our senses, our understanding of what has gone before, and our perception of our current experience to shape a likely future for ourselves. It seems like a sensible enough approach.

But there is another way. You've made a beautiful gesture to yourself by picking up this book, and investing time in exploring how you can change, grow, and metamorphose.

Like a butterfly, you recognise that your past doesn't equal your future and that your outlook is utterly limitless. People have always done the best they can with the tools they have. We are so fortunate to be living today, when more and more unhelpful frameworks for how we *should* live are being over-turned, and more of us are becoming versed in our ability to elevate ourselves and human consciousness more broadly. Today, the world really is our oyster.

Now is the time for you to savour the fruits of your meta-morphosis, the time for you to enjoy being the purest, finest version of yourself, and to revel in the delights that come to you. They'll show up the form of wonderful human connec-tions, advances in your physical, emotional, and spiritual health, and a far greater appreciation of the joys that are, and always have been, all around you.

Maya Angelou said, 'We delight in the beauty of the butterfly, but rarely admit the changes it has gone through to achieve that beauty.' Only you will know the struggle, sacrifice, self-discipline, and self-awareness that it has taken you to get here. The metamorphosis you've undergone in your inner world shows on the outside; people and circum-stances will respond to you differently from now on. Enjoy it; you've earned it.

Metamorphosis is a lifelong process. It ebbs and flows; there will be periods of incredible growth, and times to retreat back to the cocoon for a while, whatever the reason. The cocoon is there when you need it, a sanctuary from the frenetic world where you can take stock, lick wounds, nurture your family, or just be with yourself in peace.

I've been in a cocoon of my own these last few months, writing this book. Spending time in my quiet home, consuming, creating and composing, with the soft breathing of my puppy beside me, has felt like the most heavenly indulgence. I've largely shunned the outside world and social media, and spent precious time alone with my thoughts.

But now I know that the next phase is nearly upon me; the phase where I seek to share *Metamorphosis* with a wider audience. It will be different; it will feed the extrovert part of me that loves people and is energised by engagement. And that's as it should be; we're multifaceted beings who thrive on this cyclical nature of life.

Our cocoon is always there when we need a haven, but we'll find that, overall, we can serve ourselves and the world far more fully as a butterfly than as a caterpillar. Each time we return to our cocoon we'll do so from a place of greater strength, we'll use the peace it brings us to revive our energy rather than to hide from our own possibilities, and we'll emerge even more magnificent.

Fly away now, beautiful butterfly, on your wings of self-awareness and self-trust, into your wildest dreams.

A NOTE FROM SARA

Thank you so much for taking the time to read this book. I'm more grateful than you will know that you gave your precious time to read it.

If you enjoyed the book then I'd be extremely grateful if you could take a moment to review it on Amazon.co.uk. As I've published *Metamorphosis* independently, recommendations and reviews are its life-blood.

If you'd like to hear from me, **you can sign up for my Friday email: Things I Learnt This Week.** Visit www.healthywealthyandwiseuk.com to sign up.

If you'd like to prolong your metamorphosis process a little longer, be sure to check out my blog www.healthywealthyandwiseuk.com/met for free activation exercises, online resources and further reading.

Thank you, and I hope our paths cross again soon!

Sara

ACKNOWLEDGMENTS

A huge thank you to the good folks who've helped me and held my hand through this double adventure of writing, and self-publishing, my first book!

Thanks to my copy-editor, **Susan Cahill**, who finessed this manuscript, reined in my overuse of italics and exclamation marks, and introduced me to the wonderful concept of the Oxford comma. Susan can be found on reedsy.com and I cannot recommend her warm manner and thorough knowledge of the English language highly enough.

Thank you to my wonderful book cover designer, **Ged Equi**. Ged created a cover that was perfectly 'me' and managed to see inside my head.

Thank you everyone who read or listened to drafts of *Metamorphosis* and gave incredibly helpful feedback.

Finally, thanks to **Joanna Penn**, whose excellent books and generous free content provided the majority of technical know-how that I needed to publish my book independently. Her website, https://www.thecreativepenn.com/, is an absolute goldmine.

ABOUT THE AUTHOR

Sara Madderson is an author, entrepreneur, wife and mother. She was born in Ireland and moved to the UK with her family when she was ten years old. She lives in London with her husband Chris, their two children, Paddy and Tilly, and their cocker spaniel Charlie.

Before turning to writing, Sara worked in finance for a decade and then ran her own fashion brand, Madderson London, for eight years. She earned her MPhil in Early Modern History from the University of Birmingham.

Metamorphosis is Sara's first book. Given that she spent most of her childhood writing and designing clothes, she's now seen both of her childhood career dreams come true!